101
Ways To
Increase Your
Sales

PATRICK FORSYTH

**KOGAN
PAGE**

YOURS TO HAVE AND TO HOLD
BUT NOT TO COPY

First published in 1995 by Heinemann Asia, a Division of Reed International (Singapore) Pte Ltd, Consumer/Education Books, 1 Temasek Avenue #17–01, Millenia Tower, Singapore 039192
UK Edition published by Kogan Page Ltd in 1996

Reprinted 1998

Kogan Page Limited
120 Pentonville Road
London N1 9JN

© Patrick Forsyth, 1995, 1996

British Library Cataloguing in Publication Data

A CIP record for this book is available from the British Library.

ISBN 0 7494 1985 7

Typeset by Saxon Graphics Ltd, Derby
Printed and bound in Great Britain by Biddles Ltd, Guildford and King's Lynn

Contents

The Intended Reader 4

Acknowledgements 5

Introduction 6

THE RIGHT FRAME OF MIND 8

PLANNING AND PREPARATION 11

GETTING IN 18

PROSPECTING 22

FIRST IMPRESSIONS 31

UNDERSTANDING CUSTOMERS 36

IDENTIFYING NEEDS 45

PRESENTING YOUR CASE 54

HANDLING OBJECTIONS 78

GAINING A COMMITMENT 90

REINFORCING YOUR CASE 97

FOLLOW-UP AND PERSISTENCE 104

MANAGING CUSTOMER RELATIONSHIPS 109

DEVELOPING REPEAT BUSINESS 116

HELPFUL ATTITUDES 121

Afterword 128

The Intended Reader

This book is intended for those people who sell. For the most part that means the "field sales representative" rather than the broader sense of someone who sells in, for instance, a retail shop. Job titles are many and varied in this area, including: Sales Executive, Salesman, Sales Consultant, Technical Representative, and many more.

The word salesman is still commonly used as the simplest way of referring to this category of people, while excluding others (such as retail) who would logically come under the more general heading of sales person. This word is therefore used in the text, together with other terms for the sake of variety, and none of this is intended to imply that all who do this job are men. They are not. What is more the proportion of women in many a sales team seems to be growing; something that indicates that they are potentially at least as good as selling as their male colleagues, and, in some instances, better.

It is also hoped that the book will be useful to those who manage and assist salesmen; Sales Managers; Sales Directors; Sales Trainers and, in some organisations other managers also. One last category who may well find the book a useful reference are non-sales people, those who despite having a background in administration or the technical side of the company, are actually personally involved in the sales process no matter what their job title may say.

The emphasis throughout is on the practicalities of the field sales job and on proven techniques that are already working for many and which are readily available to others to take advantage of in their business. Whether you sell products or services and whatever the industry in which you work, the intention is that you will find here ideas that you can use to help you increase sales in future.

Acknowledgements

In the days when I first started work and found myself on the marketing side of the business and involved with selling, sales training was rare. There was a belief in the "born salesman" and the overwhelming majority who were not in that rare breed had to find their way as best they could. These days it is well accepted that selling is a skill that needs learning, and, what is more, that it is a dynamic process which constantly needs updating and fine-tuning if it is to maintain its edge.

During the time I have worked in marketing consultancy and training, I have run many sales training courses and seminars in a variety of industries and in many different countries. I am grateful to all those I have met along the way, those who I have accompanied, sometimes much to their discomfort, on their calls and whose experiences and thoughts they have shared with me. If I have any ability to analyse and review what works in selling it is because I have had the opportunity to observe a great deal of "best current practice". What is presented here is not therefore my pet theory of things, but is, I hope, an objective comment on what others as well as myself find brings in the business and does so most certainly.

Patrick Forsyth
Touchstone Training & Consultancy
17 Clocktower Mews
London N1 7BB

1996

Introduction

"God is on the side not of heavy battalions, but of the best shots."
Voltaire

It is said that selling was never easy and that, in the competitive market conditions that now seem to prevail worldwide, it is downright difficult. This book focuses on the need for selling to be more and more effective. It takes it as read that any chance of sales success must come from a persuasive approach and good customer relations, but recognises that competitive markets demand more. However good the product or service being sold, something extra is needed. This is because selling has become an increasingly fragile process. All may appear to be going well, and then one seemingly small factor, something handled perhaps in an ill-prepared or inadequate manner, makes a "no" more likely. Similarly, a precision in everything that is done can invest any element of the sales process with the power to edge the customer more certainly towards "yes".

The sales person who handles what they do in a way which recognises this fragility, and who understands and deploys the right mix of approaches and techniques in a way that maximises their effectiveness, gives themselves an edge in the market. Such an edge against competition will increase the likelihood of people doing business with them.

Such an edge is only available to those sales people who take a conscious view of the details of what they do. It is a mistake to believe that selling is a skill that can be successfully applied "by rote", or that like the so-called "born salesman" (who in my experience is a very rare animal in any case) we can work by instinct, off the top of our heads. The things that give you an "edge" against competition and a better chance of sales success may take only a few seconds. They may represent just a few sentences in the course of a long conversation; or they could rest on only one word rather than another being used. Whatever their nature they are always important, not least because there are few, if any, second prizes in selling, business is either won – or lost. So the details of any approach matter very much.

This book therefore reviews the sales process in this light. It does not so much attempt to be comprehensive but focuses on a number of elements – 101 in fact – all of which, singly or together, can make the difference between getting a "yes" at the end of the day, or a "no". The effect is cumulative, that is the more you get each and every element right, and right means right for this particular customer at this meeting today (a different approach and combination of approaches may be necessary tomorrow or with another customer), the more you increase the chances of success. As I once heard it put: you increase the danger of someone doing business with you.

Like an earlier book of mine *The Selling Edge* (Piatkus), which reviewed the sales job stage by stage, this book does not try to lay down the law about a "right" way to sell. However, because it is based on observation and experience of what works in a practical sense, it does intend to highlight areas that will make a real difference. You must judge, in the light of the product or service you sell, and the kind of customer with whom you deal, exactly how you deploy the techniques, but you ignore making your approach professional and appropriate in any of these areas at your peril. The most successful sales people are almost always those who work at it, and who make every detail work for them. You have to do your homework, understand your customer, plan and execute your approach in the best way you can, matching exactly what you do to the circumstances. Do that and you will leave the less aware and less conscientious sales people behind, your customers will believe they are dealing with a professional and you will do better as a result. If this book acts as a spur to the thinking and review that makes this possible, it will be worthwhile.

Sales is results orientated. Any and every method which helps achieve results needs considering. There are no rules set in stone, what works is what works. In the following pages there are 101 ways, thoughts, methods or techniques chosen for inclusion for one reason only; they can help you increase your sales.

The Right Frame of Mind

Make no mistake, the way you think about your sales job is the first thing that conditions how well it goes and what results you obtain. It is your attitude that decides how you will go about the detail of the job, and that in turn will influence how your customers see you and whether they are willing to do business with you. You are, after all, usually the only one there with the customer on the day. General attitudes are dealt with later, here we review three key approaches you can take to what you do and how you do it, all of which can influence sales results for the better.

1. Adopt the right overall approach

Let us start with an overall point and one of the considerable significance. Selling must be regarded in the right way. It is dynamic, that is, it operates against a background of change. Markets, competition, the economy are all subject to change; so are, most important of all, the customers. They are ever more demanding, ever more fickle, quick to take advantage of competitive pressures and wanting, understandably enough, value for money and service that meets their definition of both. Their attitudes may change, they are in any case all individuals and expect to be dealt with in a way that recognises just that.

What works best in selling is, as a result, not any one set approach. Selling must deploy appropriate approaches from all the available techniques and do so customer by customer, meeting by meeting and day by day. The best sales people are those who recognise this fact. They seek to consciously fine-tune what they do, they never get stuck in a rut but always approach what they do intelligently and judge exactly how to proceed in the light of all the circumstances.

This fact alone can be crucial. Because elements of the sales job are necessarily repetitive, it is easy to find things starting to be done on "automatic pilot" and that original and creative thinking about what is going on becomes less.

Selling rarely has very much to do with good luck. Sales people can however, to an extent, make their own luck; certainly they can and will do better if they see the process of working at it as a continuous one. This affects all the other one hundred points mentioned in this book, indeed they are intended as prompts to just the kind of thinking described here. In other words the person likely to be of most help to you in making your selling more effective, is yourself.

2. Be self-motivated

Every book, certainly every American book, on selling discusses the need for a positive mental attitude. No doubt this can help selling, but you cannot pick positive mental attitudes off the trees or buy them in packs of six in the local supermarket. There are, however, certain factors that do assist self-motivation in a practical sense. The wise sales person uses these to boost their thinking and assist their performance. Here we consider two areas that work in this way: *confidence* and *persistence.*

First, let us consider *confidence.* This is a question of belief, and while it is perhaps impossible to show how to create this within yourself, certainly in a short paragraph, there is one overriding principle that helps. That is to use those tangible factors on which confidence rests. For example, if you have done your homework – you are prepared – this boosts confidence, giving you things you can be sure of which otherwise might be imponderables. Similarly, knowing your product knowledge well, having clear objectives and sales aids being tried, tested and ready – all boost confidence. Bear this in mind as you read through this text and see how many of the topics reviewed can help confidence in this way.

Secondly, consider *persistence,* a topic to which we return in a number of ways in the following pages. If you do more, rather than less, if you do more than others, then you know you are that much more likely to hit sales targets. Productivity applies to selling just as much as to other areas of business.

Develop the habit of reviewing everything you do, answering one basic question! How much more certainly can you operate? And you might be surprised how much better you feel about your abilities.

3. Resolve to constantly fine-tune your approaches

There is an old saying that you can have five years' experience or just one year's experience repeated five times over. This is simple yet vital. Experience needs to be taken and, at best, its accumulation accelerated. See every call you make as an opportunity to learn something that will help you make future calls work better, operating on the principle that even the best performance can be improved. More so than any other part of the marketing side of the organisation, the sales people get the best customer feedback. You probably make hundreds of calls every year; perhaps thousands. The amount of information available from these calls is massive. Constantly ask questions of yourself. Why did they say that? Why did they voice that objection? Did they misunderstand something? Did they agree? If you can develop the habit of spending a moment replaying most of your calls in your mind after you have finished them, then you can use this analysis to gradually evolve new approaches for the future. Fine-tune the way you work and avoid getting into a rut, repeating endlessly the same phrases as if they were as relevant to all the different people you see, and what you do is more likely to remain fresh and well-directed at each and every customer.

Planning and Preparation

Most things in life that are worth doing require some effort before they return any reward. It was the hair stylist Vidal Sassoon who is credited with the saying: "The only place where success comes before work is in the dictionary"; he was correct. So do not pass over this section, believing that success or improvement will come more easily from the technique areas that follow. They can doubtless help also, and are, perhaps, inherently more interesting, but preparation is vital. It is, in fact, one of the key factors that can help you differentiate yourself from competitors and ensure a good reception from those to whom you seek to sell. A number of points here investigate the main elements involved.

4. Do your homework

No one in selling seems to like the thought of planning. You skimp it, however, at your peril. There is an old story, which I have heard attributed to a dozen different professional golfers, of them saying something to the effect that: "It's a funny thing, but it seems the more I practice the luckier I am on the day of the match". So it is with selling. The good salesperson makes it look easy, but, if they are good, then they have in all likelihood done their homework. Good luck is not to be relied on; though some say it is the reason your competitors are successful.

So *always* prepare. The salesman who does this is taking the first step to giving themselves an edge on competition. Sometimes preparation constitutes just a few minutes of thinking through before you go into a meeting. Sometimes this thinking takes place in the car outside the customer's office where a few moments reviewing their file can pay dividends. Sometimes it may mean sitting round the table with a couple of colleagues debating the best approach to take with a key prospect. It takes time, some aspects of it may seem a chore, but it should always happen. A well-prepared sales situation should conceal fewer unforeseen pitfalls, and allow greater certainty of success. The sales person who resolves to regularly spend time on preparation is making a wise decision. The next few "ways" explore particular ways of doing this.

5. Set clear objectives

There is an old saying that: if you do not know where you are going, any path will do. Every sales meeting needs clear objectives. If you do not have a clear idea of what you are trying to achieve it is difficult to set in train action to achieve it. To say the objective is to sell is too simplistic. To sell what, by when, in what quantity? And how? Many objectives may be valid. You may want simply to find out information (to allow a next stage to take place); you may want to get agreement to make specific proposals, to quote, to run a trial, a survey or a demonstration; you may want to engineer an introduction to someone else – the real decision maker. And such objectives link. A successful demonstration may lead to the opportunity to survey detailed requirements and subsequently quote on them, or report back in a formal presentation.

So clear objectives are important and they must be, as the well-known mnemonic puts it, SMART. That is:

Specific – setting out clearly what you intend.

Measurable – getting agreement to a demonstration can be measured, they give it or not, a more vague objective – "to increase awareness" – may be difficult to observe and measure.

Achievable – can we reasonably do it? It may sound nice to say we want to book their total requirement for our product for the next year at our first meeting, but is there any chance it can really be done? If a trial order is the only real opportunity, then going for that makes a better objective.

Realistic – here we must ask *should* we go for it. Sometimes we do not want the business. Maybe too large an order and production cannot cope and complaints will surely follow. Or perhaps there could be a clash in some businesses in having two major competitors as customers (they may both suspect secrets could be, perhaps unwittingly, betrayed).

Timed – this specifies when you intend something will be achieved. At the first meeting, the second, in six weeks, or a year on?

Some sales people talk of what they call "courtesy calls". There should be no such thing. There should always be a real reason – an objective – for the call, and while this is, necessarily, introspective, concerned with what we want, you should also always think of what is in it for the customer. If that is posed as a question and cannot be easily and convincingly answered, then you may need to reconsider the objective. Give your customers a reason to find your calls useful and it can be the first step towards an order.

6. Anticipate possible objections

You will know from experience that objections are not just possible, they are likely – indeed many say receiving none can be read as a sign of a total lack of interest by the customer. As your experience grows few objections should come as a complete surprise to you, you come to know the sort of thing that gets raised. Further you learn the kind of things different types of customer raise – the one who is obsessed with every last tiny technical detail, the one who quibbles over your promise of delivery. So to some extent you can, as you prepare, anticipate what a particular customer may ask; and be ready to deal with it effectively. Of course, sometimes something will come out of the blue, and always the objection may be put in a different way or, very important, need answering in a different way from how it has occurred in the past. Preparing for them does not mean you can stop thinking during the meeting or that you have a "pat" answer ready, but it will make dealing with them more certain and make it less likely that they will unbalance the case you present so that the customer rejects it. Some, you may be able to prevent arising at all by thinking ahead. Prevention may be used as effectively as cure in this area.

7. Arrange suitable sales aids

This is an area of preparation easily overlooked. There is a parallel here with the executive whose desk is habitually untidy but who always, so they say, knows where to find everything. Really? Most sales people need to use sales aids of some sort. These may be anything from a graph which illustrates and explains cost effectiveness, to a sample, an illustration, a chart, brochure or complete product demonstration – how many people would buy, say, a car without a test drive? These are used not simply because it seems like a good idea, but because the customer demands it or experience has shown it improves the ability to explain or demonstrate. If they are to be used they must be available, accessible and in pristine condition.

I once accompanied a salesman who was selling financial services. He used sales aids, and they were simple enough, the bulk of the exhibits consisting of graphs, but professionally prepared and effective in enhancing the case he made to clients. In the particular call I remember he was well into the meeting and all was going well (he was a first class salesman), he mentioned the first graph and reached into his briefcase to get it out and show the client. Three or four minutes later he was still looking; we later found the folder with all the graphs in it on the back seat of his car. The way this diluted his credibility was marked, the client said "never mind" but his face said that he found it unforgivably inefficient; and no order was ever forthcoming.

The moral is simple. Think about what you are going to need for every meeting and make sure you have everything you need with you, that it is in the right order for the particular meeting and that it is in a condition that will impress the customer. Nothing short of 100% organisation in this respect is permissible, if you want to avoid any dilution of your effectiveness.

8. Remember two heads can be better than one

By its nature the sales job tends to be a solitary one. But this does not mean that you always have to do everything by yourself. There is merit in being self-sufficient, but one must not make a fetish of it. Selling is, or should be, a creative occupation. It demands ideas and the consideration of various options in terms of action and it may be quicker, easier and that a better solution may be arrived at by bouncing the idea off someone else. The informal networks which exist around the sales team will help here, but there is another sounding board which should always be available.

This is the sales manager. In too many organisations the sales manager is rarely approached for advice because the culture of the organisation is that you only go to the manager if you cannot cope and there is a problem. If this is the case it is a great pity, it can stifle thinking and ideas, and less may be sold as a result. Now I am not advocating that you simply go into the sales manager's office and say, "Help, what do I do about this one?" (they would rightly object if this happened very often), rather that the best approach is debated between you and a solution – the best approach – sought together. This is surely only utilising the corporate resource and experience effectively and I believe the best sales managers do encourage it. If yours does not, show him this page!

9. Know your business

I was talking to the manager of a book shop the other day and he said, "Some of the publishers' representatives who come in here are just not in touch. They should be a good source of market intelligence to me, but I know more than they do about what's going on and I spend most of my time inside this one shop." Such comments are not uncommon in many industries, and are, when they occur, a considerable indictment of the sales people concerned. You have to be up-to-date on the situation, technicalities, developments – gossip even – in your chosen area of business. Anything less destroys confidence in your being an expert in your field, an image that most sales people are at pains to cultivate. Again this may take time, you have to read the trade and technical press and any appropriate literature in your field regularly, you have to talk to the right people. Your company should help. If there are things you feel you should see (a journal your customers quote to you, perhaps) ask for them. Take whatever steps are necessary, but make sure you are always seen as being on the ball in this way. Customers like a salesman who knows his business.

10. Know their business

This goes with the point above and is, if anything, even more important. You need to understand the situation within which your customers work. Not just the technicalities, clearly if you work in a technical industry you need to understand something of the technicalities, but the whole scene, the hopes and fears, the way they think. Is their business growing or under pressure, have they had staff reductions, what is their cash flow like, how important is your product or service to their business and why? There are many questions to ask yourself and being sensitive to their situation in this way will show. Some things in this area come from observation and experience, some things about large organisations (if such are amongst your customers) are public and in the city pages of the newspapers. But you can take more specific action too. For instance, many companies not only issue internal newsletters or magazines to their staff, they will send them on request to other interested parties or they can be picked up in their reception area. If so, make arrangements to see them. Reception areas are often a ready source of information about your customers, what you can see, pick up or overhear may be of real use. A friendly receptionist may also be a useful source of information.

Not only will a sound basis of knowledge be useful to you in selling, but it being observed that you take a real interest in your customers will be useful too. Your customer no doubt thinks his organisation is the centre of the universe, and likes others with whom he does business to express a real interest in it.

11. Know your product

This is vital. Some of this book was typed on a portable word-processor. It is a wonderful machine, it has changed my life and I could not now live without it. But . . . finding someone who could explain it to me, answer my questions and reassure me that I was making the right decision to buy it was a nightmare. Not only were people selling it unable to explain clearly, they simply did not know the answers to what I regarded as basic points. What is more I think this is a common complaint. On another occasion I remember sitting though a 30-minute presentation about a proposed pension scheme to the board of a company. At the end the sales consultant asked whether there were any questions. To general agreement the Managing Director announced, "I didn't think I understood any of that."

I repeat: exemplary product knowledge is vital. You need to know your product or service inside out. You need to know what it will do, why it does it and how. You need to be able to answer any question that potential customers want answered and be able to do so promptly and efficiently, and above all understandably. Putting yourself in a position like this is vital, you are always going to be vulnerable until you have the relevant information – all of it – at your fingertips. So read the brochures, factsheets and manuals and ask, ask, ask until you are satisfied with your ability in this area.

Then go on doing it to keep up-to-date.

Note:

A form or checklist may be useful as you pull together your thoughts about any particular prospect or customer. Completing such thinking before a call may be a useful discipline and need not take too long; certainly a few moment's thought must *always* proceed a meeting of any sort with a customer. Key topics to review include:

- Your call objectives
- Key points of opening
- Key points of main presentation
- Objections it may be necessary to handle
  (and answers)
- Action/decisions that you intend to prompt from the customer
- Support items needed
  (eg. visual aids, handouts, equipment, samples).

Getting In

Apart from the quality of face-to-face selling technique (certainly an area of major influence), there are only three key matters which influence sales results. They are:

- *Who you see* – which particular prospects and customers you spend time with.

- *How many you see* – selling is very much a matter of productivity – in general terms if you see more people then, all other things being equal, you will sell more.

- *How often you see them* – the question of frequency of contact is vital (too little and there is no continuity or relationship developed, too much and overcalling reduces productivity and the number of new people you can see).

Before you even consider who you see, you have to be able to take action that will result in a meeting; here we look at a number of points before getting on thereafter to prospecting.

12. Seeing the right people

Two comments are relevant under this heading. First, that in some business the potential market is way beyond what the individual can contact. For example, if you sell office equipment, photocopiers or (fascimile) fax machines, then even limiting the potential market to offices (some people have them at home), the market is huge. Secondly, which people do you attempt to see? The largest companies? The nearest? Those ones in a particular industry? And who do you see? Who uses the equipment, who has the budget, who makes the purchase decision? This might be the managing director of some organisations and a secretary in others. And, of course, they will not all need it and, even if they do, that need may already have been satisfied — perhaps your main competitor sold them a machine yesterday. Superficially they may all seem like prospects, but surely no one would pretend that they are equal prospects. Not all acorns grow into giant oak trees, most are eaten by the pigs. Even those that register an enquiry are not equal prospects either.

So you must set priorities. Sales people who allow their time to be wasted on those who exhibit no real potential, the "no-hopers", perhaps because they are in some way easy to access, will never do as well as those who accept that priorities must be set and then do so systematically.

The first guide is probably experience, never ignore the evidence of the past. Ask yourself who has purchased in the past, and why. Think through the logic of contacting one person rather than others and concentrate your activities and your efforts for example, on those which analysis shows are the best prospects. If you sell in certain areas, such as consumer products to retail outlets, this problem may hardly exist as the outlets are comparatively few in number and contact is established with them all. The incidence of new ones that need assessing in terms of potential is less. For others it is key, and their success is in direct proportion to the time and sensible thought put into deciding who to see and who not to see; at least not yet. Who you decide to see is perhaps the first decision that influences whether a sale is likely to result; so choose carefully.

13. Who is the buyer?

This may at first sight seem a stupid question. At one level you need to identify the person who buys: QED. However, *the* buyer is often, particularly in industrial selling, more than one person, or at least more than one plays a part in the buying process. It is useful to categorise the different roles that may be involved. An example illustrates the principle. Say we sell wordprocessors. The typist or secretary is the **user** and will have opinions about what they want and of any suggested option. These days the manager may well input material themselves, and so be **users** too. They also may act as **advisors** to someone who will make the decision, perhaps the administration director, if the whole company is to use common equipment. The accountant may well be an **advisor** also, at least on cost, contracts and servicing.

And if the company has a purchasing department someone there may be the **buyer** who is actually influenced by all those others already mentioned and who has, in addition, a measure of authority, large or small themselves. When the final recommendation, or short list, is in, it may be the managing director who is the **decision maker**. Having said all that the person who rings up in the first instance and asks for a brochure may be someone quite different such as the accountant's assistant.

You must never assume that whoever initiates contact, or responds to your overtures to see them is, by definition, the **decision maker**. You need to know what role they actually play, who else is involved and how the ultimate decision will be made. This may only emerge progressively as the contact is progressed, and the information about how it all works may need to be actively unearthed by active, but careful, questioning.

To add a small complication, there is another category that is worth attention and which plays a part in all this. They are usually called the **gatekeepers** and are investigated below.

14. The role of the gatekeeper

The internal role of the gatekeeper, at least as far as sales people are concerned, is probably all too clear. It is to prevent sales people wasting the time of those further up the organisation. They do however realise that some sales people are valuable, and may be persuaded to see their role as making a sensible assessment rather than fending off every caller. One thing is certain. They do not like to be treated as insignificant or dealt with without respect. Treat them carefully, ask their help, imply you can help them and their bosses and they can be an asset to your selling.

Gatekeepers are those who can provide access to others who then play a more significant role in the buying process. If a manager is the decision maker then his secretary is likely to be a gatekeeper. She may not be the only one, switchboard operators and receptionists often have a gatekeeping role. Such people may be comparatively junior in the hierarchy of the buying organisation, but they can still wield considerable power as far as the sales person is concerned. You must recognise who the gatekeepers are and then always treat them with respect. Develop a relationship, remember always to say thank you when appropriate. Show them that they are important to you, but never patronise them. Some have sharp teeth as it were and will savage any salesman who tries to use them in an obvious way. They *are* important, so saying so and dealing with them in this way can surely be natural. Remember that they will not all be junior, some people have this role though they are themselves senior. An architect, for instance, may or may not allow access to his principal who is the supremo on some major construction or development project. And, in turn, the architect's secretary or assistant will protect access to him. So there may be tiers of gatekeepers. A final point, if they are not people you meet in the automatic course of your dealings with customers, then you may need to seek them out. However you come across them they make good friends, but as enemies are no good at all for your chances of selling.

Prospecting

The balance of managing existing customers and yet constantly finding sufficient new ones to grow and develop the business is crucial in selling many kinds of product and service. Yet it is all too often something that is found difficult, distasteful and neglected; one feels there is a clear link here between these factors. It is precisely because prospecting is inclined to be difficult to fit in amongst other work priorities, and do justice to, that it must be approached systematically. Here we review something of the approaches and methodology that can make it effective.

15. Make prospecting a regular activity

There can be hardly a sales person born who does not find "cold calling" less attractive than calling on existing customers. This is not surprising. It is unlikely to be easy, the strike rate is likely to be lower and, by definition, the rejection rate will be higher. Yet most businesses need the lifeblood of a constant supply of new prospects at least to some extent. If you need a regular supply of potential new customers, then you must recognise that the activity to produce them must itself be carried out regularly. It is a common fault of many sales people that they neglect or put off action in this area, allowing an insufficient number of prospects to become a major problem. So, the first rule of prospecting is simply to do it. Set time aside every week, link prospecting to regular activities and do not let other short term pressures give you the excuse to neglect it. Do it regularly and the returns you get from it will help you achieve the results you want.

16. Create prospecting methods that work for you

Prospecting is a state of mind. It is a habit, and as such helped by cultivating a range of ways of doing it that can themselves become habits. These then can become a regular source of new leads and you do not have to think of a fresh way of producing every new contact you need. There are many ways of doing this and you need to find methods that suit you and your kind of business. The following examples may themselves be useful and may also be illustrative of how a range of different ways forward can be developed. Make a point of trying to develop more or adapting these, changing them to suit your own use.

Here are ten ways to start some thinking;

(1) Endless chain
This is simply, as the name suggests, using one prospect to lead to another. A first may come, let us say, as an enquiry. Once you know who they are, what they might be interested in, why they came to you — in other words as you begin to know something about them, you can ask who else they can direct you to.

This may be in two ways:

- asking: "do you know anyone else who might be interested . . .?"
- analysing: "If this bank manager is interested, which others can I talk to?"

(2) Centres of influence
These are people or organisations through whom you may make contact with numbers of prospects on a regular basis, because they have the power to introduce or recommend. They may include trade and professional bodies, chambers of commerce, associations, banks and others. It is worth thinking through which may be useful in your business, listing them and systematically keeping in touch to ensure they know of you, they know something about what you do, and are reminded of this and kept up-to-date. (Share the task of keeping in touch with colleagues, each taking responsibility for a number of such contacts.) Any contact which can lead to numbers of new customers is likely to be both worthwhile and cost effective if contact is maintained systematically.

(3) Personal observation
This should never be underestimated. If you develop the habit of being observant then a regular supply of new prospects can

follow. First, consider things in print. You need to review regularly any journals, newspapers or publications of relevance to your business. Trade or industry journals are a good example. So are in-house newsletters if you have major companies as customers who produce them, and, yes, they will often put you on the list — provided you ask. News of companies, developments, staff changes, relocation and more can all provide information to lead you to a new prospect. Secondly, keep your eyes open and check anything that might help you. Ask yourself: who has moved into the new office block on the corner? or into the office next door to someone you already visit? — again such observation (and perhaps a little associated research) can lead to new names and thus new prospects.

(4) Chance contacts

This is closely related to personal observation, but worth a separate mention. I have twice obtained work following a conversation with someone sitting next to me on an aeroplane, when idle chatter — "how much did you pay for your ticket?" and if it was cheaper than yours "where did you buy it?" — identified common business interests. I once even got work from someone whose office I wandered into, lost, to seek directions in the bowels of an office block. Beware, of course, of taking this too far, but keep an eye open for such opportunities, particularly in places where people of similar interests meet — a trade association meeting, perhaps.

(5) "Cold canvass"

Simply knocking on doors is probably not to be recommended to anyone but the least faint hearted. However, one variant may well be useful. In places where different businesses exist close by, such as on an industrial estate or in an office block, it may be worthwhile knocking on some doors near to an existing visit; not to try to sell them something, but to discover names. Ask the receptionist who is in charge of office stationery, travel or whatever. Again, even a few new names may be useful and they will be geographically convenient too which aids productivity if you subsequently need to visit them regularly.

(6) Lists

Not so much the big ones like *Yellow Pages*, but the small specialist ones. Association membership lists, interest groups, sports clubs; whatever ties in with you business area. This can yield names for small mailings, and can be made manageable by being reviewed progressively with mailings following at so many per week. Some research on what lists exist is often worthwhile.

(7) Past clients/contracts
If you are systematic there should be few of these. Despite that there will likely be some. People have good reasons sometimes for stopping doing business with you, some that have nothing to do with you; someone leaves the company, a budget is cut, expenditure is delayed — there are many reasons. If so always check when things may change again, note it in the diary, however far ahead, and remember to get in touch again and keep in touch as appropriate during any enforced gap. Of course, if you have **not** been very systematic in the past, it may well be worth a comprehensive research of the "archives".

Note: A customer for one product in your range but not for another, may be persuaded to buy both. One hotel discovered it could boost its restaurant trade by mailing the business clients it met, who were recorded in a separate file and previously neglected.

(8) Suppliers
Anyone you do business with might be persuaded to do business with you if your product or service is something they buy. You know them. They know you. They doubtless want to retain your business, so they are unlikely to reject out of hand a suggestion to talk.

Furthermore, you will no doubt have a good record of such people in your accounts department, and need to do little more than check through the invoices they send you to identify them.

(9) Extra curricular activities
Business and pleasure do not always mix, but sometimes they do. A good number of business deals really are struck on the golf course just as legend would have it. It may be worth reviewing what you do, where you go, what clubs or associations you belong to, and seeing whether you can get more from

them in a business sense. This is worth a thought but definitely to be the subject of care, after all the committee may not approve (though if you were on the committee maybe you would make more contacts).

(10) Directories
There are so many directories published that, certainly in the UK, there is a directory of directories. This implies there could well be one or more that is useful to you, that you do not currently know about. Check it out, even one with some good new names can be useful.

17. Be available

One salesman I know had been trying repeatedly to get to see what he felt could be a major prospect. Always there was an excuse, but never an outright refusal; so he persevered. Finally the prospect agreed to see him but "only if you can be here at 8 am on Thursday", and the prospect knew full well this would entail a very early start and a two hundred mile journey. However, it was agreed, and at 8 o'clock they duly met; at nine my friend took the first of what was to be many orders from the customer, and received an apology for the early start: "I had to test the service your company gives" he said, "if you were prepared to be here punctually at such an inconvenient time then I think I can rely on you."

The moral is to be available, when and where the customers want. If someone works to a pattern that makes them receptive early in the morning or late at night, or on a Saturday or . . . whatever. If you are prepared to be there, perhaps when others are not, this alone may make a difference and give you an edge. Time is of the essence for many these days, I regularly find myself conducting training programmes at weekends when a company does not want to eat into business time. Fine, if that is what they want, that is what I will do. The principle is the same.

It is a principle that applies not only to meeting them but also to contacting them. If they say ring during the evening or at some other odd hour, then that is when you ring. And you may need to be contactable also, and there is a panoply of modern devices to help: answer machines, mobile phones and message services. Now it may seem that I am advocating working 24 hours a day, seven days a week. Not so, most customers are, in fact, fairly conventional. They will want to see you during normal business hours. The few exceptions you can cope with without disrupting your whole life, and you may find that the extra business that can come from being more readily available to them than your competitors is well worthwhile.

18. Stand up to prospects

During my training work I find myself talking, with varying degrees of formality, to many different groups of people. A typical course may be attended by between 12 and 20 people, and other kinds of event may involve many more, sometimes, at a company event or conference, I find myself addressing 100 or more people. However used you are to public speaking, it is always a somewhat traumatic moment when you start a new presentation. Everyone has his own ways of combating nerves and his own way of making himself as comfortable as possible with what he is doing, but one thing I remember surprised me early on when I first began to do such things. After feeling apprehensive at standing up, I found that it is, in fact, more difficult to do if you remain seated. In training, for example, this is true even when a group is very small. For most it is easier to inject the necessary clout when on your feet.

What has this got to do with prospecting? Well, a major method involves telephoning, however the contact has been originated, however the name found and whether or not there has been some other form of contact first, a letter sent perhaps, a telephone call is an important part of the process. Making such calls can be awkward, there is a certain — embarrassment is probably the right word — though it is the uncertainty of the outcome and the possibility of rejection that makes it difficult.

There is one way of reducing this feeling, and I suggest this in all seriousness (it brings laughs as an idea if I mention it on courses), and that is to stand up when making such a call. Before you dismiss this, try it. It works. Somehow if you are sitting at your desk it is much easier to begin: "Excuse me, I am so sorry to worry you, but perhaps I could . . .", when you are searching for, and need, a much more punchy start. On your feet the adrenalin flows to a greater extent and somehow it is more natural to be a little more forceful.

I know it seems like an odd idea, and I will not apologise for that: it works (and is also appropriate for that other difficult category of calls you may sometimes have to make to chase up debtors).

19. Use prospecting systems

An enthusiast for time management systems is supposed to have once asked the great scientist Einstein why he did not use them. "They are so useful," he said, "you never lose track of your ideas." The great man shook his head. "But I have only ever had three good ideas," he said. Most of us are paid for having many more, albeit smaller, ones, and it is a wise man who never trusts anything crucial to memory. If you have the details of a dozen products and maybe several hundred customers and prospects buzzing round in your head, it is simply unrealistic to believe you will retain every last detail. Write it down (advice I will not apologise for repeating more than once as we go through the book). You do not want to forget names you have found and action you have planned — "I'll ring you again towards the end of the month" you say, or in two or three months — and you have to be 100% certain of doing it. And not only for your own benefit; promises must be kept and it can be impressive when they are. So whether it is in a diary, notebook or — these days — an electronic organiser, note every name, every number and note also specific action — when you will telephone or call and when, if necessary you will do so again, and again.

20. Making appointments

Of course, there are people you can see without an appointment, and types of selling where appointments are not the norm. However, there are good reasons to make them wherever possible and signs also in most markets that customers are increasingly reluctant to see people without the visit being pre-arranged. First, appointments being a high proportion of calls tend to make sales people more productive; you see more people. Secondly, customers like to be dealt with this way and that may be reason enough.

Appointments can either be made for a regular call, either

specifically or in principle. For example, a salesman calling on retail accounts may arrange to see someone at 3 pm every Tuesday. Alternatively, he may agree just to call on a particular day — the second Thursday of every month perhaps. Other appointments are longer term, but can still be made, at least as a general commitment, well in advance. An agreed quarterly or even annual review meeting may be arranged, a telephone call nearer the time being used to confirm and set an exact time.

Other kinds of appointment making are more difficult — cold calling or even following up a prospect's request for more information. A real initiative must be taken and it helps if such a call (they are almost always on the telephone) abides by certain rules:

- Open clearly and positively.
- Have a reason for calling that you can describe in customer terms to show what is in it for them.
- Have a reason for setting a meeting (rather than some other action they could take) perhaps something they will see.
- Talk about the meeting as working *with* the customer, do not sound as if you want to do something to them.
- Suggest alternative times, the first more specific than the second: "how about 3.30 on Wednesday afternoon, or would sometime on Thursday or Friday suit you better?" Keep offering times in pairs of alternatives.
- Do not give up if they cannot see you in the next week or so, an arrangement 3 weeks or 3 months, or even a year ahead, is still positive interest.

And finally consider confirming in writing and check all appropriate details (do you have the address, is there parking, etc.).

21. Do not base your approach on a lie

I once saw a company appraisal form on which managers were asked to mark their subordinates from 1 to 10 on a list of characteristics and performance factors. One of the entries called for a mark for honesty. This seemed to me to be a nonsense. In business, at least at the level of subordinate, you are either honest or you are fired. But there is that convenient in between: the so-called white lie.

There may well be a place for these if life and relationships are to work, but sales people have some much used phrases that are so transparent as be to the equivalent of putting up a big illuminated sign that says "This is only a ploy". Consider some examples:

- "I will be in your area on Thursday" – rubbish, it means they will be there if the prospect agrees to see them. And even if it were true it is not a good reason to offer a new prospect; why should they be concerned about your con venience?
- "I will only take ten minutes of your time" – rubbish, it takes some salesmen this long to get the formalities out of the way and get down to business. Customers just see this as a line.
- "I can only make this offer today" (or to you) – and it sounds as if you say it to everyone, every day.
- "I was recommended to contact you" – by who? often this just means that the prospect's names is next out of the directory.

It is all too reminiscent of the old buyer's response "If I believed that, you would be able to sell me the Great Pyramid." You can no doubt think of more and may, perhaps, even think of some you are inclined to use that are similar in texture. Customers are not fooled for a second by such phrases. They will just be seen as a sign of little or no preparation, having no clear objective and not treating them with respect. Avoid this sort of start to any conversation.

First Impressions

To use an old cliché: you only get one chance to make a good first impression. Its truth makes it worth repeating. If you get off to a good start, everything else you will do thereafter during a sales interview will be just a little easier. A good start affects the customer and it affects your confidence. It does not just happen, it starts with preparation and then needs to be actively worked at to ensure you achieve the impact you want. And it is worth going for, it makes a real difference, as the points here demonstrate.

22. First impressions last

Everyone, if they are honest, knows the temptation of making snap judgments about people. We all tend to do it, and, what is more, such impressions tend to be both firm and yet often inaccurate. So it is with others and ourselves. You should therefore give no excuse for the wrong impression to be formed about you. This links back to preparation. If you are well - prepared then you should be more confident, better able to make a good start. This is not a question of gimmicks or an overdone approach, but of being business-like and aware of the need for everything to go well early on – having such an intention is the first step to achieving it.

Things like a greeting, links to previous conversations, and stating a clear, benefit orientated reason for calling, all help (the concept of benefits and their use is dealt with in detail later). And even before this a display of appropriate manners, waiting to be asked to sit down or not smoking unless it is obviously not going to cause offence for example, is also necessary. Of course, things become more relaxed as you get to know a particular customer and visit him regularly, but such courtesies should always be borne in mind and do have an effect on how a customer will react early on.

23. Looking the part

It is common sense to look the part, and be smartly turned out. In this book which will be on sale in a variety of parts of the world I would not presume to lay down the law about dress. Suffice it to say that prevailing standards are best followed, so that a suit matters most in England, whereas only a shirt and tie will normally be worn in, say, Singapore. It is always important to be clean and tidy. Again some businesses set their own style, with someone selling, say, design or advertising services dressing in a more avant guarde fashion – but if in doubt as to the conservatism of your customer, do not overdo it; it is perhaps better to be less fashionable and make a sale than vice versa.

What you must certainly do is look efficient, and that is influenced by many things, all of which you need to think about in advance. You may look personally fine until you open your briefcase and the inside looks like a rubbish dump. It does not even matter if you can find everything, it will effect your image for the worse. This principle includes being kitted out for the job in hand. For example, if you call on farmers you may need a pair of wellington boots in the back of your car, and if you demonstrate machinery you may need overalls. There are some too who put their faith in what is called "power dressing", believing that if you have the right tie, the best shoes and the correct accessories, then this makes all the difference to your image. There may be some truth in this, however, I heard of one salesman telephoned out of the blue by a prospect. "One of your competitors has just been to see me, and as I noticed he parked a Porche outside, I think I could do with another quote." So do not overdo it.

24. Starting as you mean to go on

Getting off to a good start is not simply a question of impressions, there is a very business-like aspect to it, one that lasts throughout the meeting with the customer. Consider: only one person at a time can truly direct a conversation, one leads and the other tends to follow. This does not mean there is no give and take, and it does not mean that one party is subservient, but one does lead and in selling there is merit in being the one that does so. Whether you successfully get hold of the meeting and grab hold of it so to speak, depends on how you act. Certainly it must be done in a way that is totally acceptable to the customer.

Two points here help. First, watch that a chatty start to the meeting, a part of the proceedings for which you have no real plan, does not lead to the customer chipping in with something that leads you in what is, for you, the wrong direction. Make no mistake, however, meetings do take a moment to start; we need to go through some ritual of getting started, we talk rather pointlessly of the weather, the difficulty of the traffic or where to park until someone says: "Right, let's get on, can you tell me . . . ". If the customer makes this switch then it may be difficult to get back on track, and the initiative may have been lost. If you contribute a more relevant start, it gives you something you can deal with and move away from to the business of the meeting.

Secondly, one technique that works well in many kinds of selling is to suggest an agenda for the meeting. This does not need to be stated as more than a helpful suggestion. It can be modified in discussion, but once agreed it allows you to proceed very much along the lines that suit you, indeed it provides an element of control throughout the meeting as you refer back to it and move on to the next stage. The early part of any meeting is a key stage both to your confidence, you feel and thus operate better if you get off to a good start, and to the control and direction of the meeting. Resolve to sell from the driving seat.

25. The manner most likely to succeed

The overall manner deployed most likely to make selling successful can be characterised by the inter-relation of two factors. These are projection and empathy. Projection encompasses everything about the way you come across: power, personality, weight, authority, expertise – what is sometimes called "clout". Empathy is the ability to put yourself in someone else's place and see things from his point of view. Both are important, but it is the way they are put to work together that creates the right impression. Too much of either holds dangers and the diagram below shows four classic arrangements. This is not intended as an academic view of things, but can provide a measure of how you are coming across, which, if you keep it in mind, can assist you balance as you go along. Because in many cultures the sales- man is viewed with at least some suspicion, adopting the right

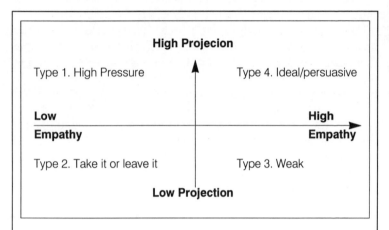

Type 1 – the "high pressure" sales person is over aggressive and insensitive. *They* may feel they win the argument but, in fact, their projection, without empathy becomes self-defeating and switches people off. The archetypal high-pressure person is the popular image of, say, the insurance salesman.

Type 2 – the "take it or leave it" sales person has little interest in the other person, nor his own ideas. A lack of commitment to the whole process tends to let it run into the sand. The archetypal take it or leave it person is the kind of unhelpful shop assistant with whom most of us are all too familiar.

Type 3 – the "weak" sales person is one who "means well". And so they do. They have good sensitivity to the other person, come across as essentially nice, but take the side of the listener so much that persuasion vanishes and they achieve no commitment.

Type 4 – the "ideal" sales person is seen as having a creative understanding of the listener, being well-informed and produc- ing both agreement and commitment to the satisfaction of both sides. Being seen to see the other person's point of view is, in itself, crucial.

Figure 1: Factors influencing the manner of sales approach

manner, one which makes sense in terms of what customers want from suppliers, makes very good sense.

It is possible to categorise four distinct types of sales approach on an axis of high and low projection and high and low empathy – the balance here is important (see Figure 1). Both elements contribute to getting the manner right, either can be overdone. Keeping this balance in mind and actively working to get the mix right will help you be persuasive while being seen by customers as a reasonable person with whom to deal.

26. Use eye contact

In most cultures avoiding the other party's eye is regarded as shifty. Yet the first stages of the sales meeting are such that they do present some psychological difficulties. You wonder what the buyer thinks of you, you worry as to how it will go, you have a good deal to concentrate on to try to make sure it does go well; all may hinder an open approach. Yet if you can look the customer in the eye and develop an easy manner to go with it, then you are much more likely to give the right sort of impression.

Much of the impact eye contact has is to do with the amount of time eye contact is maintained. Less than one third of the time can result in you being read as untrustworthy. More than one third of the total time with eye contact tends to indicate interest in the other person, which is just what a customer expects from a sales person, so ideally to build reasonable rapport you should be in eye contact 60/70% of the time. When eye contact drops below the level of the other person's face, a less formal atmosphere is created. And looking away completely, slow blinking or closing the eyes for longer periods than normal can be a clear indication of lack of interest or, worse, boredom.

A final point, gestures can direct eye contact. Pointing to something you are showing a customer directs his eyes towards it, lifting the head and engaging eye contact again will change the emphasis of the meeting. Such points are part of what is called body language and, while this is not a science nor is it able to offer infallible signs, it can be useful and may be something worth investigating separately.

Understanding Customers

Without customers, preferably satisfied customers coming back for more, you will make no sales. They are all unique, competitive markets make them increasingly fickle and they are often difficult – though there is an old saying "No customer is worse than no customer" – or at least require some understanding. Understanding them does not just make your job easier, it is inherent to the whole process of a customer relating to a sales person in a manner that plays a part in prompting them to do business with you. The points here focus on this key part of the sales process.

27. The need for understanding

Customers expect that sales people will understand them; really understand them. And they do this in two ways: first, they expect sales people who deal with them and people like them on a regular basis to be well-briefed about their industry, product, kind of business – whatever is appropriate. Remember what was said about "homework" earlier. You should take active steps to make sure that your level of knowledge in this way is beyond criticism; I have even had calls in the past myself from salesmen who have not even taken the trouble to find out what my company does, yet still seem surprised if this is commented upon and a request for a meeting refused. Of course you will never know as much about their business as customers do themselves, however you must know sufficient to do a good job and as much as customers expect you to know. Without this you will simply not be taken seriously and, at worst, you will lack all credibility. Of course, the basis of such knowledge increases with time and experience; at least it should do – we all should learn from experience. The good salesman makes a point of it.

Secondly, you have to add to the background knowledge you now possess with additional information about each customer's current circumstances and their specific needs. This can only become clear progressively as the meeting and the relationship progress, and needs active noting of what is volunteered and active probing to find out more (the latter will be discussed under the heading Identifying Needs). It is these two kinds of information about customers acting together that provide a powerful basis for what you do at the meeting. There is an old saying that information is power. In selling, customer information and an understanding of it is a most necessary tool and excellence in this area can differentiate you significantly from competitors.

28. The power of empathy

Empathy is the ability to put yourself in the other person's position and see things from their point of view. It may be your natural instinct, or you may regard it as a skill to be developed and deployed as necessary throughout the selling process; or a bit of both. Whichever may be the case, empathy is vital and it has already been mentioned under the earlier heading about manner. There is an additional point about it, however, which is worth taking on board. You do not need just to be empathic, to take in and appreciate the customer's situation, but to do so in a way in which your doing so clearly shows. Customers must *feel* that you understand. Many kinds of selling have, or can benefit from having, an advisory connotation, and this may be something that customers demand or appreciate when it is offered. You may be advising on what, from your range of products you feel is most suitable for the customer, or you may be acting as a problem solver, analysing some aspect of your customer's business and making recommendations linked to your product. In either case empathy is a necessary part of the process. For example, someone selling computer systems is very much in this last category, and someone selling computer stationary can be, by selling smooth operation and efficiency rather than simply refilling the stationary cupboard. When customers say of a particular salesman ". . . he's a good person to do business with . . ." empathy is almost certainly one of the characteristics they have in mind.

29. Respect customer's views

Never assume that customers will see everything the same way as you do. The world is full of different people and they all have differing views, ideas, prejudices, and in some cases some or all of these may not be the same as your own. So be it. You can agree to differ, but you have to work with customers. You do not have to like them (though it is nice if you do get on with most of them, and certainly you need mutual professional respect) but argument is not the best basis for a good customer relationship. This is especially true of business matters – it may matter less if you support different football teams. Attitudes to their company and product or service, to the standard of quality or service, to finance or time – your perspective on all of them may be different to theirs, but taking their view in your stride may be vital. Unless you can understand their view of, say, financial matters you may never be seen as the sort of person to buy from, even if your product suits them.

30. Working with customers

This is a simple, yet effective, point. Customers do not like to be "sold to". In many cultures the image of the sales person is not exactly as we might wish it. We want it seen as professional, at worst the customer views the salesman with suspicion, seeing him as a low level, unprofessional con-merchant who will use any trick to sell even inappropriate goods to the unwary if it will swell his commission.

The historic reasons for this do not really matter, for the most part such an image is actually long outdated, if it does linger on your job is simply to dispel it. A number of things can be done to help and will be referred to in this book, one is certainly the concept of working *with* the customer. You should talk about this specifically, rather than giving any hint that you view the meeting as an opportunity as doing something to them. Expressions like: "Let's go through this together" and "Let's take some time to work this out together" give the right feeling and the right description to the transaction. Using this kind of phraseology will help you set the right tone to particular meetings and go a little way to dispelling any of the old myth about the insensitive, high pressure salesman if it exists.

31. Customer types

Customers are all important, but they are not all equal. And what I mean here is the size, actual or potential, of the business they do, or may do, with us. The nineteenth century Italian mathematician Pareto gave his name to what is called *Pareto's Law*. This is what has become known as the 80/20 rule; in sales it means something like 80% of your business comes from 20% of your customer lists, and this may be true of revenue and profit. The figures are not likely to be exact, but all but the most atypical organisation is likely to exhibit this pattern – so, incidentally is an individual sales territory. Most organisations recognise this and will categorise customers into several groups, A, B, C, and D for instance, which reflect size. Some may be judged too small to deal with direct economically and, as a result, their business may be put through wholesalers or agents. There may be numbers of reasons for categorisation in terms of systems, organisation and so on, however, the key point here is that different customers need different treatment.

It is not just that customers are best dealt with a little differently for our convenience, it may well be less economic to service a smaller customer in the same way as a larger one, but that some larger customers *demand* a different and, of course from their perspective better, level of service. This is perhaps most obvious in consumer markets where the large retailing groups expect higher discounts, more regular delivery, longer credit and possibly a long list of other things: special promotions, packing, assistance with merchandising, etc. But it is true in all businesses, consumer, industrial or service. If decisions are well made in this area, and the right package of service and representation is directed at each category, then the success with each will be better. This has got to be done in a way that links revenue (or potential) to cost, and thus margin, and which tries to match, so far as possible, the needs of both parties. The days of dealing with every customer as if they were all the same has long gone for most, though none of this implies ignoring the smaller customers. They may only bring in around 20% of the business but no one wants a 20% drop in business. They too have to be looked after. Matching your approach to customer size in this way can pay dividends.

32. Types of buyer

While all customers are individuals and must be treated as such, there are types of buyer just as there are types of any other category of people. Sorting such categories in the mind is perhaps a good start to being able to deal with all the different types of customer you meet in the right kind of way. It provides a manageable basis for dealing with the decisions involved. The following is not intended to be definitive, you may well come across people who do not fit in any of the following categories, but it provides a basis for planning and maybe for devising additional categories of your own.

Certainly, it is possible to categorise customers, at least in a general sense and in a way that helps you to get off on the right foot with them, and run a better meeting thereafter. The sort of way this is usually represented is shown in the figure below contrasting just two differing factors on two axis reflecting customers' attitudes and approaches to buying and sales people.

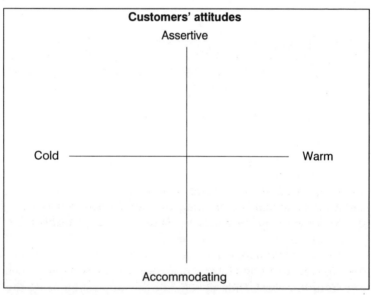

Figure 2: Types of buyer

This produces a list of four types, and they are sufficiently different to demand different approaches. This is perhaps best described with reference to their likely differing attitudes to sales people, stated below, in quotes, as a customer might describe them.

Type 1: (assertive – cold)
'Sales people cannot be trusted. They are determined to sell me something I neither want nor need. I must therefore be tough and resistant. The best defence against sales people is offence.'

Type 2: (accommodating – cold)
'Sales people cannot be trusted. To defend myself I try to avoid them. I stay as uninvolved as possible.'

Type 3: (accommodating – warm)
'Many products I am responsible for buying are very much alike. Since it doesn't matter to me which one I buy, I prefer to buy from a sales person I like and who likes me. I like to try to make friends with all the sales people who call.'

Type 4: (assertive – warm)
'I buy things which have been demonstrated and will benefit me and my company. I buy from sales people who prove they can help me, by offering products and a quality of service which exactly satisfies my needs.'

How to open a sale with type 1 (assertive/cold) customers

- Do not expect a warm welcome.
- Accept their negative attitude, and use your professionalism as a foil.
- Keep small talk to an absolute minimum.
- Emphasise that you are there for sound business reasons.
- Make your opening remarks short and very much to the point.
- Do not be intimidated.
- Do not try to be clever by using what these people will consider sales people's ploys'.
- Appear to let them take the lead, but demonstrate your *control* of the interview by attentive listening, note taking, and asking concise, factual and open questions, which will, in fact, help direct the meeting.

- Be firm and polite but never appear subservient.
- Position yourself as confident, professional and calmly determined.

How to open a sale with type 2 (accommodating/cold) customers

- Expect these people to appear cool and distant, and under stand that you will be seen as a threat to their security until you have won their trust.
- Be calm, professional and unhurried.
- Avoid pressure tactics.
- Do not say too much during the opening moments of an interview. Let them 'size you up' for themselves, and do not cloud their picture of you by being flashy, brash or pushy.
- Some small talk is recommended.
- Do not expect to make a sale on your first visit to these people.
- Position yourself as an adviser.

How to open a sale with type 3 (accommodating/warm) customers

- Expect a warm welcome, but understand that these people welcome everyone: their warmth does not necessarily mean you are particularly special.
- Allow them to express their feelings with some small talk, but stay in control and do not let them lose sight of the fact that you are there for business reasons.
- As these people like to feel they belong to select groups, mention as early as possible the involvement your company has had with other comparable, reputable companies.
- Tell them exactly how you would like to structure the interview, including your role and theirs.
- Do not appear too officious or clinical by producing brochures or samples too early, or by taking too many notes: keep the opening conversational.
- Position yourself as a friendly purchase recommended.

How to open a sale with type 4 (assertive/warm) customers

- Expect a correct and professional greeting with a firm hand-shake.

- Take your seat unhurriedly and prepare openly for the interview by taking out of your briefcase the documentation – including a notepad – which you will need.
- Demonstrate your own professionalism, and understand that these people will expect your acknowledgment of their commercial skills.
- Your opening remarks must be natural (not contrived), short and clearly indicate that you already know a fair amount about their company.
- Do not be dogmatic: they will want you to be flexible so that their ideas and objectives can be accommodated in a *joint* solution.
- Be prepared to revise your call objectives.
- Avoid a fixed or rigid 'standard interview' approach.
- Position yourself as a creative, experienced problem-solver.

Respect of the customer's individuality, taking an accurate view of what 'type' of customer you are dealing with and making a real attempt to 'get on their wavelength' early on in the proceedings will always help you in any meeting. Sales technique is not, after all, something to be applied slavishly or by rote, but something to be deployed intelligently case by case. And the variable that dictates exactly how that deployment should vary is the customer. Every customer is different, and it is a dangerous mistake to treat them as if they were all alike.

Remember also that, at the prospect's office, you are on their territory. You should respect it. It sounds obvious enough, but do not sit down until asked; do not even ask to smoke unless it is clear (perhaps because an ashtray is on the desk) that this is not likely to offend; do not bang your hard briefcase on their polished desk; and do not get too close, people do not like being crowded – so respect their space.

Be considerate of anything and everything that will indicate a caring manner, one that respects the customer, their views and their property. They will appreciate the attitude this displays.

33. Respect and use customers' names

Names are peculiarly personal. You did not, in all likelihood, choose your own, but you do like people to get it right and remember it. Using names actually changes the feel of a phrase; consider the difference between:

- "Right, Peter, what I suggest we do is . . . ."

and:

- "Right, what I suggest we do is . . . ."

The feel of each is different.

In many cultures the habit of remembering and using names is weak. So a few pointers and your developing a real intention to get it right may be useful:

- listen carefully whenever you are introduced or someone says who they are
- if it is not clear ask again, and if necessary ask how to spell it. Remember people would rather you got it right and were interested than made mistakes or asked again later
- make a point of using the name in the conversation, not so often that it becomes pedantic, and maybe a little more early on to help your memory
- always use the name as you leave or conclude a conversation
- make a written note of names at the earliest possible moment, and record also other associated names (eg, the buyer's secretary)
- consider carefully when you use the more familiar form of someone's name, too soon and it may offend, too late and they may consider you over formal. (Remember the old line, "My name is Smith, John Smith, but you may call me 'Sir'.")

People do business when you get down to it, not companies. You can increase the personal feel you give your own company too: do not say "I will get the service people to contact you", rather quote a name: "I will get Mr . . . .". So make every contact as personal as appropriate, and this will give a better feel to the conversations that follow.

Identifying Needs

Ready, aim and fire is a logical order of action for both the military and those in selling. If preparation equates with "ready", then identifying needs is certainly likely to improve the aim. Being "on target" in selling means having a clear understanding not just about customers, but relating to their specific and individual needs. Of course, some of these they tend to tell you, but often only briefly, or partially. The selling job demands good investigative skills, it is by no means only about putting over your case and demands not the "gift of the gab" alone, but also the ability to ask questions, to do so in the right way, and to listen to and use the answers to better target the sales approach that you then design to follow. The following points investigate this topic.

34. What customers want

Customers have two prevailing feelings when buying or considering buying from a particular salesman. The first is that they are the important one in the relationship. You sometimes hear salesmen talking about buyer's support, as if there was some reason why people should do business with us just to help us. This is wrong. There is no reason in the world why they should support you; they will do business with you if *they* decide it is in their interests to do so and only then. So they are right to see themselves as important and the way in which they are handled in terms of courtesy, efficiency and appropriateness must reflect this.

The second feeling they have is of even greater significance in successful selling. They want the salesman to consider their needs, and consider their needs to be unique, if only in detail. Selling was described earlier as "helping people to buy". It is a good definition and suggests strongly that a knowledge of what customers want, exactly what they want and how they want it is the basis for success in selling. Recognising this is the first step. Of course, you have to find out exactly what needs a particular customer has, and use that knowledge to increase the effectiveness of your sales approach.

35. Need identification techniques

While it is essential that you try to find out from a customer his needs, questions must be carefully asked. First, because the majority of customers are busy, and do not want you subjecting them to a time consuming Spanish Inquisition style of questioning. And secondly, because you need to find out certainly and accurately, indeed it is task which, successfully achieved, helps you differentiate yourself from competitors. Just how much you can differentiate and how important that is will be reviewed later in this section.

So how do you go about this questioning? There are several factors that will make what you do work well. Questions need to be:

- accurately phrased: if a question is not precisely phrased it may bring the wrong answer
- mostly *open-ended*: that is questions that cannot be answered by "yes" or "no". Thus "tell me exactly how you plan to use the product? is better than "Do you see a cost advantage?" The first gets them talking, which is why open-ended questions work best, and the second, while it may be answered "yes", which does give you some information, may well leave other reasons for considering using the product unstated. Open-ended questions are likely to be the best way of getting what may well be the considerable amount of information we need, and are most likely to make the process most acceptable to the customer. Close-ended questions (those that can be answered "yes" or "no") can be used to vary the conversation and verify more specific details in checklist style
- *probing*, that is using a series of linked questions which dig deeper and deeper to pursue a particular line and establish fuller understanding. This is an important technique and warrants reviewing in some more detail.

There are four levels of questions that can be used:

1. Background Questions: these produce the basic detail, what kind of company is it? how is it organised? what is its budget? – whatever the required areas of information may be.

   Then there are two probing levels, usually called problem and opportunity questions (though the problem level need not always focus on the negative).

2. Problem Questions: these start to show what area of activity the product or service being reviewed is to fit in with.

3. Implication Questions: these pursue the point raised at the previous level to see exactly what the results of any purchase will be.

4. Need Questions: this is where you want to be, focusing on the need.

An example makes the principle clearer. Imagine the beginnings of a conversation between someone selling business travel and a possible client: questions like "What destinations do you travel to most often? which class do your people usually fly? how frequently do they go?" are all background questions and provide a useful start to the information gathering.

Then a question like: "What particular problems do you see affecting your travel plans over the next six months?" takes things to the next layer. Let us assume that the questioner discovers that keeping costs down is making it difficult to service new markets in the Middle East while maintaining the frequency of contact which current export markets demand. Useful information and if followed up by an implication question "How is that likely to affect things?" – "Well, I suppose it will slow progress in the Middle East", puts the questioner on strong ground. Finally, a need question focusses the customer's mind: "So, if I could show you a way to maximise the frequency of visit and hold down costs, would that be of interest?" – "Yes, indeed". If the salesman can then do just that, perhaps suggesting extending some of the visits to nearer markets to include flying on to the Middle East and thus maximise fare utilisation, the customer will surely take notice.

Never skimp this finding out process. If it is well done it makes everything you have to do during the remainder of the selling process easier. And if you are in competition and do this better than they do, you should have an edge on them throughout the rest of the process.

36. Listen to what the buyer says

Listening is important when conducting a sales meeting. This is reviewed here as it is clearly especially vital when questioning to identify customer needs is taking place. You will look at least careless, and at worst incompetent, if you say something later in the meeting that makes it clear that you have not been listening properly. It is actually easier said than done, there may be many distractions and your mind is necessarily on a number of things at once, what to say next, what to ask and so on. There is an old saying that mankind was made with two ears and one mouth and that that is the right proportion in which to use them, so you must listen carefully and that means what is called *active* listening. Some ideas about this follow, in checklist style:

Active listening to obtain information

1. **WANT TO LISTEN** This is easy once you realise how use ful it is to the sales process.

2. **LOOK LIKE A GOOD LISTENER** If they can see they have your attention, customers will be more forthcoming.

3. **UNDERSTAND** It is not just the words but what lies behind them that you must note.

4. **REACT** Let them see you have heard, understood and are interested. Nods, small comments, etc. will encourage.

5. **STOP TALKING** Other than small comments, you cannot listen and talk simultaneously. Do not interrupt.

6. **USE EMPATHY** Put yourself in the other person's shoes and make sure you really appreciate their point of view.

7. **CHECK** If necessary, ask questions to clarify matters as the conversation proceeds. An understanding based, even partly, on guesses is dangerous. But ask diplomatically, do not say "You did not explain that very well".

8. **REMAIN UNEMOTIONAL** Too much thinking ahead ("However will I cope with that objection?") can distract.

9. **CONCENTRATE** Allow nothing to distract you.

10. **LOOK AT YOUR CUSTOMER** Nothing is read more rapidly as disinterest than an inadequate focus of attention.

11. **NOTE PARTICULARLY THE KEY POINTS** Edit what you are told to make what you need to retain manageable.

12. **AVOID PERSONALITIES** It is the ideas and information that matters, not what you think of the person; this can distract.

13. **DO NOT LOSE YOURSELF IN SUBSEQUENT ARGUMENT** Some thinking ahead may be necessary (you listen faster than they talk, so it is possible); too much and you suddenly find you have missed something.

14. **AVOID NEGATIVES** To begin with at least, signs of disagreement (even visually) can make the customer clam up.

15. **MAKE NOTES** Do not trust your memory. If it is polite to do so, ask permission.

All the above will help you listen more and miss less; and both can make a difference.

37. Making notes

A great deal of information can be obtained in a short time with effective questioning techniques, too much to trust to your memory; however good you may think it to be. You must make notes as you go along. The need for this is compounded by the fact that you often do not know in advance which bits of information will be useful as the meeting progresses, the relevance of specific points may only become clear as the meeting progresses. In some meeting situations it may be appropriate to ask for permission before writing down much of what a prospect says. It seems so obvious, but many have walked out of a meeting and immediately had to say "What was it he said?" – so make a note. Got that?

38. Agreeing needs

Finding out what customers want, exactly what they want and why (and keeping a note of it), is important. However, it is one thing for you to find out, and find out accurately, what your customers want, it is another for them to know that you have done so. Unless they are aware that you have an accurate picture of their requirements they will not be able to have the same confidence in what you say or recommend. In this case the usefulness of what you have discovered will be reduced. The answer is to agree with the customer that the needs are true reflections of what the customer has said. This can be done with simple questions: "Is that right?" – "Am I understanding you correctly?" Alternatively, it can be done by summarising: "Let me just be sure I have got this right, what you are saying is . . .", listing the key points that have emerged. This makes sure you are correct, and it makes that accuracy of understanding clear to the customer. It also allows you to refer back to points in the right sort of way when they are referred to again later in the conversation. It will give a better impression to the customer to say something like "This will give you the cost effectiveness you said was so important . . ." when you refer to the way your product or service will suit them, than if you say: "This will be cost effective, which I am sure you will appreciate . . .". In the latter case your own certainty may be justified in the case of cost effectiveness, something most people want, but it may well be unwise to make too many assumptions about more specific matters.

39. Two kinds of need

There are more customer needs than the rest of the space in this book could list. Some are generic; many kinds of customer want value for money, transport or to save money. Indeed the same product can be bought by different customer for very different reasons. The needs one person has for the product may not be even remotely the same even for very similar customers. Consider holidays as an example. The same resort may be chosen to provide a romantic honeymoon, to indulge in sporting activities (and that *is* two reasons), to meet old friends – or make new ones, to work quietly, to impress the neighbours, or get away from them. Or . . . no doubt many more.

Such needs may be tangible or intangible. For example, a new car may be bought to fit in the garage (a tangible need for something less than a maximum size); or because it has good fuel economy which can also be measured. Or it may be to meet a need for an aspiring businessman to look successful; or a younger person to look trendy, both of which are more difficult to specify.

There are two key implications here for the salesman. First, do not overlook intangible needs. They can be very important to people and may not only be overlooked, but are sometimes not taken seriously by sales people who do not share the need or even understand it. Secondly, and perhaps more importantly, intangible matters can become deciding factors when competing products are very evenly matched, and buyers search for something to assist them to make a final decision. It may be that the potential car buyer wants both fuel economy and a car sufficiently small to go in the garage. He still finds that there are several models that meet both these requirements (and no doubt others), and even after extending his specifications to include still other factors, a four-door design and front wheel drive perhaps – there are still two possible models. At this point, he may well be influenced towards a final choice by something intangible such a preference for a certain colour or the overall image, which are much less objective judgments. If you recognise that this stage is being reached, then selling must focus as much on the intangible as the tangible; perhaps exclusively so. In taking steps to identify needs both kinds must be sought and the implications to the possible course of the sales conversation recognised.

40. Identifying and agreeing customer priorities

Before the identification stage is complete, you must ascertain something about customers' priorities. This is important because their various needs often seem straightforward but can, in fact, be in conflict. For instance, a customer may say clearly that they want a service supplied fast, to high quality and at the lowest possible price. Now this may be unrealistic from any supplier, with something fast and high quality being relatively expensive, and something less expensive taking longer to supply. Which factor is, in fact, the most important? Superficially the answer may be that all three criteria are important. Further questioning can discover that, if a choice has to be made, then cost is most important. Or perhaps timing is the key and the customer's attitude to cost will change to achieve what they want in this area. Just as with needs themselves, the identified priorities can be agreed with the customer and any reference back made in their terms: "So, your priorities will be met, achieving supply ahead of the deadline and . . .". As your product or service will only be acceptable to the customer if it meets their priorities, this identification is crucial. Without it everything else done can be off target, if it done accurately the case you go on to describe will fit in neatly with their requirements.

41. Using record cards

Although record cards should be originated early on in any relationship with a new customer, and act as a reminder of basic details such as the customer's name and address, their use goes far beyond this simple role. They can help ensure that your approach is accurately directed, tailored to the needs of every individual customer. So the record card will, if made to contain the right information, act as a checklist to remind the salesman of a multitude of facts about the customer. Without doubt customers want an individual approach, they want their particular needs met and believe that these are unique. Perhaps they are, if not small differences between the requirements of one customer and another will be important to them. It is very easy to pretend that we retain every detail about something so important as a list of customers, but most people do not have perfect memories. You really do need a written record of any facts that will help you sell more effectively, and a check, albeit brief, of the record card should be made a mandatory action prior to every call.

Having touched on the subject of record cards, some of the other topics that can usefully be used to record are listed here:

Customer's name, address, telephone number (and fax)
Contact names and job titles
Account number
Source of original lead

Record of business done (product mix and value)

Call frequency and timing

Personal details (customer preferences – even their birthday)

Geographical details (where exactly are they, can you park easily nearby)

Customer organisation background (subsidiaries, other locations, etc)

Financial details (discounts, etc)

Potential and trends

You can no doubt extend and refine this list with your own business in mind. Remember, as you do decide what to record, that you are creating a *company* record (they are only your customers on behalf of the company) and the degree of detail is, in part, dictated by what others need to know. A morbid thought perhaps, but ask yourself what would happen if you had an accident tomorrow and someone had to pick up the thread. The information recorded should make this as easy as possible.

The record card is a useful aid to sales effectiveness and sales productivity. Do use it and, of course, keep it regularly up to date.

Presenting Your Case

This is the heartland of the sales job. Whatever else needs to be done, and whatever else may exert influence over the degree of impact you have, there is a major job to be done here. It is here that you must be most clearly persuasive, yet there is more to it than that. Whatever you must do to put across your case (this can include description, illustration and demonstration) must be done carefully in a way that increases the power of the picture you are building up in the customer's mind. You must also continue to differentiate, as it is here that customers are making their most direct comparisons with your competitors. Always assume there are competitors, and never assume they are anything but professional. The factors reviewed in this section are all directed at increasing the sales effectiveness of what you do in this central area of your task.

42. What it means to be persuasive

Customers want to make a buying decision their way. They want to think about whatever proposition you are making to them, they want to assess it and make what they would regard as a considered decision. Their thinking is designed, however consciously to weigh up the case — see next page — putting many points of differing import on the scales as it were to see how the whole picture stacks up (and, of course, if they are comparing you with competition then it is two or more such balances which they will look at).

The thinking involved can be characterised as follows, in a sequence first formalised by psychologists in the U.S., which you will find mirrors a common sense analysis of what goes on in the buyers' mind (think of your own thoughts as you contemplate some purchase).

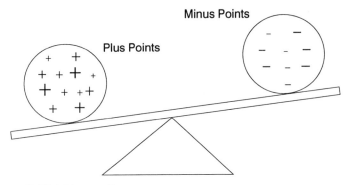

Figure 3: Weighing up the case

Buyers say to themselves:

- I am important — they want to be treated as such
- Consider my requirements — they want to be dealt with as a unique individual
- How do I know your proposition will help me? — they want details, explanation, etc
- What are the facts? — they want to put together a picture that enables them to make a decision
- What are the snags? — nothing is perfect, and most purchases involve compromise, so these points must be discovered and added to the balance
- How do we do business? — they also want to assess how it will all work, who will they deal with, will things be delivered on time, what about service, etc.
- I agree — but only if their analysis leads them to that conclusion.

A sales approach must take this thinking into account and match the thinking — selling is helping people to buy, but it must also be persuasive, your approach must work for you as well as fit the prospect's thinking. So what do we mean by "persuasive"?

In sales terms we can define "persuasive" as an approach which is seen by the customer as understandable, attractive and convincing. None of these on their own is enough to secure business, and together they must not only make a strong case to the customer, they must differentiate your case from competition and do so powerfully enough to make you, your product and company, first choice. As we have seen selling must be based on customer needs, and identifying these is a priority; using them is a priority too. There is no point in asking the customer a great many questions and then manifestly not appreciating their situation as you go on to explain in detail what your product or service offers. In most fields of selling customers expect a tailored approach. So perhaps the first rule is that your approach must be individually tailored to give each and every customer what they want, an approach which they see respects their point of view, which matches their needs and so generates more immediate interest.

Bearing this in mind will get you off on the right track and will quickly show the reason why needs identification and preparation are so important. But this is a complex stage, there are many separate things to be done yet the whole stage must proceed smoothly; this is important to your personal positioning, if it is handled smoothly, if it appears well thought out and relevant (because it is!) then the customer will conclude he is dealing with a professional and take more serious note of what you say.

43. Making what you say understandable

It is probable that more sales are lost because of lack of understanding than for any other more complex reason. This is not simply true of technical products and services (though they may present special challenges) but of all areas of selling. And the reason is simple; communication is not easy. The chances of misunderstanding is ever present between two people with different backgrounds, experience, intentions, prejudices and points of view. This may involve the different interpretation of one word — for example, just how fast is immediately? The salesman may mean that he will see to something when he is in the office tomorrow morning and get the details in the post that day. The buyer may assume he will have the details on the fax within the hour. Alternatively, it may be that a long disjointed explanation of, say, the cost advantages a product offers ends up confusing rather than informing.

So the first rule is probably to be careful, not falling into the trap of thinking that communication is entirely straightforward, but making sure that you choose words carefully and make sure that you work at being clearly understood. What else helps? I would mention four factors:

Structure: the logic of a message is crucial. This means taking things one at a time, in bite sized pieces that both you can deal with manageably and that the customer can comprehend, and flagging or "sign posting" what is being done. Thus something that begins "You will want to know something about how we can meet your needs, what costs are involved and how quickly we can train your staff to use the equipment. Let's take your needs first, and I'll say something about reliability, then . . ." is likely to be followed more easily than something which just jumps in and deals with points at random. If the customer knows what is coming and feels it will be what he wants to hear he will be more receptive, indeed knowing your initial thinking is clear and appropriate impresses and gives some advance credance to what is to come.

Sequence: this goes logically with structure. There needs to be a clear and relevant sequence to the way that you go through something, and again this should be clear to the customer. For instance, a hotel sales executive selling conference space, a job that entails showing a prospect around the facilities, may sensibly elect to take them round — and describe things — in the sequence of a participant at the potential conference, starting with the reception, moving to the conference room, on to where coffee breaks will be taken, then lunch and so on, taking in the equipment that will be provided along the way. Every sales meeting needs thinking about in this sort of way to make sure that one, two, three does not become two, three, one.

Visual aids: something visual always makes things easier to understand. The hotel sales executive has the whole property to act as a visual aid, but very much simpler things have the same effect. A picture is worth a thousand words the old saying has it, and there is a great deal of truth in it. A graph may make a point about cost effectiveness in a moment that it might otherwise take many minutes to explain; photographs, charts, samples, brochures, all these will help you get your message over. See what is available. Create more if necessary; and use them.

(More of this in point 52)

Description: Do not just tell them; paint a picture. Some sales people rarely use an adjective, yet it is essential that people see what you mean. You must stir their imagination. The paint surface on a car is not "shiny", it has a "silken finish"; an employer will perhaps not buy an incentive scheme for his company that will be "nice" for employees, but he may be interested in something that makes them "believe you are the best employer in the world". While you need to beware of becoming cliched, it is worse to sell yourself short by failing to create a real picture in the buyer's mind and thus generate fuller understanding.

In presenting your case, this aspect rightly comes first, understanding is the foundation upon which the rest of the selling process rests.

44. Beware of jargon

Nothing dilutes understanding more easily than inappropriate use of jargon. Jargon is professional slang and is particularly used in context of technical matters. Between people of like understanding it is useful shorthand. Within my own firm no one has time to say "all comers' seminar" (that is a training event promoted by, say, a management institute and attended by people from several different organisations) so we say "GT course". It stands for general training course — and no, I have no recollection of how or why it started — but we all know what it means and using it saves a second or two. It is meaningless, however, to our clients and such a phrase must not be used externally or it will cause confusion. What is worse you may not detect such confusion. People do not always react at once to such a phrase. They do not interrupt and ask what it means (not least because they may fear they should know and do not wish to appear stupid). They let it go by and hope the overall sense of what is being said remains clear. But if it happens very often they notice, and quite possibly their understanding is reduced, or they do get lost, have to ask and resent the need to do so. Either way your credibility suffers.

So watch out for jargon, especially as for most people its use is a habit. It comes in two varieties: company and industry. Company ones such as I quoted above, are things — often reduced to sets of initials — to do with products, systems, processes, people, departments, all the things to which reference is made often and where a shorthand description is therefore useful. The technicalities of an industry are also prone to jargon. Some more than others. Computers are a case in point. The machine on which I prepared this book is a marvel of modern technology. But the manual has a nightmare lack of clarity. The language in it seems to be 50% jargon and assumes that the user has a particular level of understanding that makes this appropriate, although it would be perfectly possible to write most of it in plain English. This makes a good final point: the important thing with jargon is not so much to avoid all the technicalities, but to make sure — absolutely sure — that they are pitched at an appropriate level for those to whom you speak. In addition, some phrases become so hackneyed that they lost all meaning, I asked a friend in the computer world what exactly the phrase "user friendly" meant. He thought for a moment, then said: "I suppose it means it is very, very complicated, but not as complicated as next year's model!"

45. Talk benefits

Customers do not buy products and services for what they are, they buy them for what the products or services do for them or mean to them. They do not buy precision drills (what they are), but the ability to make precision holes (what it will do); and they will only want that because of some deeper need, to repair the car or put up shelves. This is probably the single most important tenet of successful selling, yet the world over there are salesmen talking predominantly about features (things that the product or a part of it is) when they should be talking benefits. And, as a result, there are buyers with their eyes glazing over saying to themselves "So what?"

Talking benefits, and indeed leading with benefits, is key in making what you say attractive. It is not so complicated, yet perhaps because so many people were trained about the things they sell from the starting point of features — "these are the things about it", it takes a conscious effort to state it that way round.

The first task is to recognise which is which, feature or benefit, and it is useful to think through your product/service listing benefits first and seeing how they link with features. For example: a car may have a 5-speed gearbox (a feature), telling the customer this may seem just like another piece of technical information prompting the response "So what?", worse the inexperienced driver may worry that it is more complicated than he can manage. If the salesman has identified a need for economy, he can talk first about low fuel usage and money saved (benefits), quoting the feature of the 5-speed gearbox as a reason for that being possible. One feature may, of course, link to more than one benefit. In the case of the car, reduced engine wear and smoother high speed cruising may also result from the 5-speed gearbox. All product description can be handled in this way, thus a grill may be better described as being able to cook a dozen eggs at one time rather than saying it has a surface area some 300 square centimetres. Saying something about how it will cook not only allows a benefit to be described, it is also a much more descriptive way of putting it to anyone involved in cooking — they can then see in their minds eye how much easier that will be than the smaller model they have now.

Talking benefits in this way as you describe product, company, people and service that support them is a vital part of the sales job. It is important to get it right, and an area you may wish to explore in more detail than there is space to go into here. (If so my earlier book *The Selling Edge* — a Piatkus paperback may make a useful reference.) Figure 4 is reproduced from another book: *Marketing on a Tight Budget* (Piatkus), and sets out an example of how analysing the product and arranging notes about the various aspects of it can act as a useful checklist to help you produce more natural benefit-orientated conversations.

Remember all customers are different, and in some cases you may be selling to a group of people who *all* influence a decision, as with a board of directors. In either case people will have their own needs and agenda and benefits must be presented so that they relate to these individual situations and points of view.

Figure 4: Benefits and feature examples

Family car

Need	Low cost – not expensive to run
Benefit	Good miles per gallon figures
Feature	Efficient engine design/fuel injection/aerodynamic profile

Venue for a wedding reception

Need	Memorable
Benefit	Wedding photographs that people will love
Feature	An attractive eighteenth-century country house hotel with beautiful gardens

A cooker

Need	Must cope with the family
Benefit	Will grill six steaks at one time
Feature	A 200 square inch grill pan

An accountant

Need	Cost-effective
Benefit	The right work with no disruption and at minimum cost
Feature	A computer-assisted audit

Note: This approach also reduces the likelihood of using too much confusing jargon. For instance, digital circuitry may make a roving telephone more efficient, but that description is both a feature and jargon. Saying it is crystal clear and will work equally well in every room in a large house, because of the digital circuitry, starts with features, uses the feature to add credibility and is truly descriptive.

46. Relating benefits to individual customers

The tailored nature of the sales approach has been mentioned before. Linked to benefits it is vital. It is one thing to define what the various benefits or features are, but that does not mean you have to throw all the benefits at every customer. Two things are important here: suitability and comprehensiveness. First, think about suitability. In the example of a motor car, fuel economy was shown as a benefit assisted by the feature of a 5-speed gearbox (this is not the only contributor to the level of fuel use, of course). However, the usefulness of this benefit depends on the individual customer being interested in economy. Someone buying a high performance, prestige car such as a Ferrari might well not care how far it goes on a litre of petrol, though he could be interested in other benefits produced by the same feature — high speed cruising being more comfortable in a fifth gear. So benefits must be selected intelligently to match customer needs and priorities.

Secondly, consider the need for comprehensiveness. I once called on a customer accompanying someone selling research services. Early on in the meeting the customer asked: "Perhaps you could give me some background about your company?" — "Certainly", came the reply, following which the salesman did not appear to draw breath for 35 minutes. He described chronologically the company history, its start, development, ups and downs, the people, clients, services ad nauseum. Each piece of information was well described, it was all true, but most of it was simply not relevant to the client, who had probably expected 35 sentences, or even words, rather than 35 minutes. Comprehensiveness is never, or very rarely, an objective; achieving comprehensiveness just takes far too long. Customers are busy people and they expect you to concentrate on what is most important — to them. You must have all sorts of information at your fingertips in terms of benefit, but you must then select from it, picking those benefits which you judge are most likely to make the case you want and using those, in the right order and the right way to achieve what you want. Do this and your proposition will seem more attractive to more people.

47. Deploying different types of benefits

There are three different types of benefits and each presents different opportunities to make what you sell appear attractive. These are:

- *benefits to the person in his job;* thus a system being sold to an Accounts department might be described as: ". . . something that will eliminate order processing errors".

- *benefits to the customer as a person;* saying perhaps: ". . . and it will stop people complaining about order processing errors".
- *benefits to others who are important to the customer;* thus, bearing in mind links with customer service you might say: ". . . customers will reliably get exactly what they order".

Using the full range of benefits available and relating them to all possible types of need can increase the power of what you say. So too can combining this sort of statement into a logical sequence so that all the listener's needs are met. For example: "With this computerised shelf allocation system, the best mix of products is fitted into the space available (*benefit*). This means you will get continuous sales of the high volume lines (*benefit*). Overall you optimise sales and profits from the available space, whatever it may be (*benefit and need satisfaction*).

The more you work with the concept of benefits the more adept you will become at putting things in the terms with which customers most readily identify.

48. Offering proof

In defining persuasion, the third element mentioned was making what is said convincing, credible to the customer. Most would appreciate the truth of the fact that the customer has a certain skepticism towards anyone selling. They believe the salesman has a vested interest, they believe that they need to be skeptical and if a good point is made about product or service, their first reaction may be to think: "They would say that, wouldn't they". So they want proof. The main form of evidence, certainly the one that builds in best to the benefit orientated conversation you should be conducting, is the features. Well selected benefits on their own reflect customer needs. Benefits followed by features reflect needs and offer linked proof, as in a statement such as: "This model will give you the low fuel consumption you want and reduce your motoring costs, because it has a 5-speed gearbox". There is factual, physical proof here; the customer can see and touch the gear lever, and is reassured that it really exists and is not just a salesman's ploy. Such proof may be asked for and, even if it is not, should be built into the argument you are putting across as it is an inherent requirement of the buyer. Never rely solely on your own argument, build some real proof into the case you present.

49. Testimonials and references

More proof may be needed than can be provided by features alone (see above), and in particular customers may demand that this is from some outside source, independent of the salesman. Here you may need to do some assembling of the kind of point that can be made to offer external proof. There are different independent authorities to be quoted in different product fields. For instance all the following are sources of independent opinion and thus provide proof:

- the star rating or Travel Bureau award given to a hotel or restaurant
- a motoring organisation's independent test of a car's fuel consumption
- sales figures may have this impact: the most popular brand
- experience similarly: twenty years of making product X (and the time can be independently checked) may well mean something in terms of quality or reliability
- reviews of a book.

You can probably think of more examples, and need to think systematically about your own product or service.

A further and sometimes more powerful form of proof is that of testimonials or references. In other words past client or customers. Even general mention of the kinds of people you already deal with to a potential new buyer may be reassuring. Specific past names quoted may be more useful. Remember you may need to get permission; are other customers happy for their names to be mentioned? Is any confidentiality involved? And select carefully. Quoting to a small company that you do business with several large multinationals may put them off, and vice versa. Similarly if you quote a company which is competitive with another this may just annoy them, and if they are so dissimilar that they feel they cannot compare this may add nothing.

The right supporting evidence of all sorts, fielded in the right way is powerful in adding credibility. Have the right evidence ready and use it wisely.

50. Checking progress

The stage of any meeting when you are describing your product or service is one when, perhaps necessarily, you will be doing most of the talking, but you should not be doing it all. You need to have some feedback as the meeting progresses to check that you are on target. It is easy to let your enthusiasm for getting across your message make you talk uninterrupted, yet the customer will not value a monologue so much as a conversation in which they are involved. They appreciate your checking periodically whether you still have their interest and whether what you are saying continues to be relevant. This is something easily done, in part, by observation. Obvious signs of acceptance or rejection you will see at once, provided you look for them. Nods, expressions and manner will all provide clues as to what reaction you are getting. But you need more than this, your conversation has to include checks such as: "Does that make sense?", "Should I give you more details of that?" Such questions need not be complicated, and if some of them are open questions, that is the customer cannot answer them with a simple yes or no, then you will obtain actual comment as to how they are feeling. Asking, for example, "How well does what I am saying tie in with the kind of approach you have in mind?" Not only is the feedback valuable, the information provided is like having a hand on the tiller in a boat, enabling gentle changes of course as the voyage progresses and as conditions change along the way. The whole process improves the accuracy of what you do and the likelihood of an order resulting from it.

51. Summarise progress

Perhaps an extension of checking progress is the technique of summarising. This is always useful, but the longer a typical sales meeting is for you and the more complicated it may be, then the greater the need to keep it well organised. If you are directing the meeting and proceeding in a clear, structured manner then the customer should keep up with the argument, however summarising briefly as you go along will help make sure everything remains clear throughout. You do not want to give the impression of extending the meeting unnecessarily, but you do need to recap, especially on topics that are important. This can be done as a help to both parties and sign posted as exactly what it is: "Let me just summarise at this point, it seems there are three main criteria that have to be met, first, . . . ". Or you can just make it a part of the conversation. In either case it will help keep the meeting on track and help you keep things straight in your mind. Keep the customer with you in this way, it can help keep them with you right up to the moment they say "yes".

52. Managing sales aids

The need for sales aids was mentioned earlier. Here we consider their use, but first how do you store them? In a word, carefully. So many times I have been with sales people who have either not been able to find something they have said they will show the customer, or who have pulled it from a brief case that looks as if it contains the aftermath of a small explosion, looking as if the last place it should be is in front of a customer. Such inefficiency will be noticed and sales aids are important, they deserve to be looked after.

They also deserve to be used correctly and the golden rule is simple; you must let them speak for themselves. If there are two things many sales people find difficult, they are being patient and keeping silent. And the good use of sales aids demands both. For example, if you are using a graph, it must first be introduced. This introduction should explain why it is being shown, in other words what it will help explain to the customer — why he will find it helpful. Then you show it. And you wait. You wait until the customer's attention comes back to you from the graph, because, if the thing is of any interest at all, then when it is put in front of them they will look at it and it will take his attention. He cannot look at it, concentrate on it, and listen to you at the same time. So you wait. And the more complex or the more interesting it is, the longer you must remain waiting. This may seem a simple point, but because it can seem awkward to keep silent there is a great temptation to chip in and continue the conversation. But if you do and if what you say is an important point, you may succeed only in distracting him from the graph and yet not do so sufficiently for him to take in the point you have just made. After a moment's hiatus the conversation resumes and not as good a total point has been made as you would have wished. This scenario is made more complicated if you have a whole brochure to go through, every time you turn over a page then you must wait for the customer to take in what he sees and for his attention to return to you.

On the other hand, the effect of seeing something at a sales meeting is powerful. It makes things easier for the customer to understand and this, of course, they notice and value. It paints a picture, and it can save time — a commodity that the customer will value. It also adds variety to the meeting which helps maintain concentration, and can appear very person-alised. Something may be shown to the customer as what is clearly part of the standard sales material, something all or most customers see. Nothing wrong with that, the customer will expect the salesman to be well equipped in this respect and likes to see that he is. But there is sometimes an opportu-nity for material to create a different impression by being (or sometimes seeming to be) tailored just for this one customer. This may come in the description: "Knowing we would need to talk through the figures, I prepared a graph that will . . .". Or it may be visually tailored, material prepared using the customer's figures perhaps, or a note to be left with them which has their name or company logo on it.

Good sales aids can help make the customer find the meeting memorable. It pays dividends to make sure that you have the right number of them, that they are good quality and appropri-

Exhibits/ Equipment needed	To relate to the customer's situation	To show the product in operation	To prove the claims we make
1			
2			
3			
4			

ate — genuinely helpful to the customer — and to use them carefully and effectively.

Note: So important is it to get things right in this area — the right aids, appropriately organised — that you may find it useful to check through what you plan to use on a checklist. The form shown on page 67, or something like it, may assist this thinking.

53. Do not exaggerate

This is a most important maxim. Never, ever exaggerate. Nothing switches a potential customer off more quickly than exaggeration, do not be tempted to do it. One phrase too many and your credibility collapses around you, in fact of all the mistakes you can make in selling this is . . . but you are right, I am exaggerating. Though I hope to make a point.

Seriously, credibility is a fragile flower and a good case can very easily be diluted by something that strikes a potential customer as "over the top". If you have good product by all means say so, but give reasons for excellence and spend more time talking more about what the product does for or means to the customer than about simply the fact that it is good. Beware particularly of superlatives. If you say something is the best then you must be able to back it up. Too strident a description from which you have to climb down: "Well, when I say best, I mean undoubtably one of the best . . . " will dilute any good impression you may initially have achieved. Remember the skepticism with which much of what anyone with something to sell is received, and that customers question each statement, asking themselves whether it should be taken at face value, whether it is to be believed and deciding whether the case being presented is becoming stronger or weaker. Finally, remember also — a common mistake — that few things are "unique" (a much overused word meaning literally like nothing else); and that being quite, very or entirely "unique" is simply grammatically incorrect and a misuse of a word which is powerful when correctly used.

54. Do not pressurise

Customers like to make a considered judgment to buy. Pressure to make a decision before they have completed what they regard as the necessary thinking process, weighing up the pros and cons of a potential purchase will often have the reverse effect of that desired. It will increase their resolve to think it through and not to be rushed. Pressure is usually read in three ways:

- as insensitivity to the customer's point of view (this is particularly bad because one of the things they pos itively seek as a characteristic of sales people is under standing of them and their point of view)
- as a smoke screen for some product weakness, which they feel will show itself in time, hence the inappropriate rush to close the deal
- as desperation, which might have all sorts of causes– none of which inspire confidence in a buyer.

So go for every sale by all means, push hard, be persistent, but do not put undue pressure on the customer in a way that will be obvious and which will be read as unprofessional.

55. How to demonstrate effectively

Not every product lends itself to demonstration, but many do. And when they do an effective demonstration can strengthen the overall presentation considerably. Seeing is believing and there is no substitute for a customer actually having the evidence of their own eyes to back what the salesman says. But demonstrations must be approached in the right way; they must be effective and that means 100% effective. Anything less simply does not meet the need.

An effective demonstration starts with consideration of who you are demonstrating to, it may be one person, it may be many. A group presents some of the problems of a formal presentation. You may feel exposed standing in front of an expectant group, and thinking beforehand about what you will say and how you will make the talk go more smoothly and boost your self-confidence. Is the decision maker there? or are you talking to someone who will make recommendations to someone else? This may be important to how you direct things, similarly, and perhaps more important still, are you talking to the user? If you are demonstrating, say, an office machine — a fax perhaps — who will use it? Some at the demonstration may want reassurance that they can work it easily, others may want only to check that their staff can do it, or think about cost.

A successful demonstration needs preparation. Whatever you are going to demonstrate must be in good order. You must have everything you need at hand and — if possible — have checked out, if you are going to the customer's office, where you will be. Have you sufficient space, will you be near any necessary electrical point, will everyone be able to hear you, are there likely to be interruptions? In your own office or showroom all should be set up in advance, but make sure it is.

What are the key factors? Well, many of the basic rules of selling apply, you must focus on needs, maintain interest (not all features may be of interest and a comprehensive demonstration may be neither necessary nor appreciated), go through to a pre-explained structure and sequence and, above all talk benefits. With that in mind, remember:

- **set up fast:** make sure you can get everything ready quickly, better still get the customer to leave you to get ready on your own. You may have to do things they would not have to, like get a machine out of its box or change an electric plug, but if it takes too long it is still likely to be read as inefficiency.
- **make it understandable:** this is vital. Demonstrations are all too often spoilt by jargon, gobbledegook and confusion. Everything must be spelt out so that it is crystal clear. Being easily understood will be read as a good sign for their own straightforward use of whatever you are demonstrating. On the other hand if you get in a muddle then people will immediately assume that if you find it complicated (though dealing with it all day) then they will find it very complicated.
- **it must work!** If whatever you demonstrate does not work, does not work first time or only works with difficulty then you have a real problem and, from the customer's point of view, quite right too. Everything must work and work perfectly.
- **make them feel they can do it:** if you are with people who will use the machine or whatever it is, make sure they feel able to do it. Better still let them do it and prove to themselves that they can cope with it easily. This may involve not just demonstration but training, prepare how you will do it, take your time and get it right.

- **project what you want:** and what they want, if the demonstration must stress quality, cost effectiveness or ease of use make sure this is a prime message that comes over.

Throughout the process the emphasis is perhaps on proof. You are not just talking about it, you can show it, they can try it and seeing is believing. But you must work to ensure everything goes exactly as you want. There are very few second chances in selling and in few parts of the process is this more true than in demonstration. Time spent to get it right is time very well spent.

56. Making terms and conditions clear

Many businesses have contractual terms of varying degrees of complexity. Sometimes there are factors within them which customers do not like, however much they understand the necessity for them; cancellation arrangements are perhaps an example of this. Because of the perceived difficulty in introducing such topics, it is easy in selling to avoid facing such issues, the thinking tends to be that it is better first to concentrate on obtaining an order and then worry about the terms of business. But this can cause problems. Customers can feel that issues have been disguised or avoided rather than delayed and you need a clear policy as to how you deal with such issues in your business. This does very much need to be tailored, every business is different in the way they operate, but some general pointers may still be useful.

The existence and use of any terms and conditions must protect the financial position of the supplier and, in particular, protect profitability. At the same time it is important that:

- they are communicated clearly and prevent misunderstandings
- they project efficiency
- they enhance the customer relationship
- they encourage conversion of business effectively and promptly
- they link to any other necessary arrangements and documentation

In discussing terms and conditions never apologise for their necessity. Stress the *mutual* advantages, talk about working together and if necessary use a checklist to ensure you deal with everything systematically. Specifically you may want to evolve a step by step way of introducing, describing and making terms and conditions stick. The following illustrates the kind of progression involved:

Introduce the concept of contractual agreement

You need to consider the timing of this in your business, but it is usually best early on rather than later, and though details may be left over, it is important to make it clear that "contract" means something confirmed in writing. Remember the moment passes; it may get progressively more difficult to introduce contractual matters later once it has been left too long. Do not wait for the customer to raise the issue. He is unlikely to do so. And link mention of the contract to the written offer.

Make clear the details

You must be careful to spell out accurately the detail and should not assume the customer is familiar with everything — even if they have dealt with you previously.

Stress particularly figures and timing

There must be no misunderstanding about the details which, in the worst scenario, can cause the greatest problem. For example, are costs inclusive of tax? When is "in a month's time" exactly? (four weeks or . . .?). Two factors are of particular importance:
  – deposit policy/timing
  – credit arrangements

Check understanding

This may be as simple as an occasional "Is that clear?", but is very important. It is no good, at a later stage, believing everything was straight — between you — you need to know.

Document your side of arrangements

Tell the customer what you will do, and follow it up efficiently and promptly in a way that sets the pattern for clear to and fro written confirmation. And make it easy for the client. Administrative chores breed delay, customers may prefer you to summarise details of a discussion so that they can write a couple of lines that say "that's right". The reverse will take longer.

This may be checklist led, in other words the details that need to be documented come off an agreed checklist document which acts as a prompt and reminder; it can be all too easy to overlook apparently small details.

Ask for confirmation
Whatever it is you want, written confirmation, a signed contract, (the agreed internal policy specified) you need to ask — specifically — for it. It is not necessary to go round the houses, you do not need to make an issue of it (the customer does, after all, see it as a business arrangement and will not be surprised), but you do need to make the process, and implications clear, and get it underway.

Record the action
Keep a clear note of what you have done, how the customer has responded and — most important — when it needs checking and when further action is needed. This should clearly link to follow-up diary systems or be, infallibly, a part of the more sophisticated computer data base and "prompt" systems so many use today for their customer records and information.

Chase for action
This is crucial. If the customer ignores key stages, and some will, you must actively remind them of their commitment. Do not feel awkward about doing this; after all you should be following up agreed commitments ("when will you let me have the contract back?" "by the end of the week") so customers will expect it, and besides the penalty for delay can be very damaging. Such chasing must therefore always be systematic, courteous, but insistent.

Adopt the appropriate manner
Throughout the process make it clear that this is not a negative procedure, indeed ultimately it can be presented as a protection for customers. So deal with it in a way that is efficient, and implies good service, that is professional and positions yourself as an appropriate point of contact from the customer's viewpoint.

Link to follow-up
The contractual arrangement links to all stages of the sale and afterwards. The supplier must deliver "on the day", this is their part of the contract and all the service issues are important here.

Further we should see the process described as linking to:

- **invoicing**, and here it is most important that the invoice **accurately** reflects the agreed detail (and customers seem to find so often this is not the case), and is straight forward and clear. This may best be submitted with a personalised covering note linking to obtaining feedback and to the future relationship. Sending the invoice, of course, implies chasing to get it paid. Again not an easy — or palpable — task, but it must be done and it is frankly easier to follow up in a way that gets it seen as a routine, rather than only when so much time has gone by that the approach must be heavy. This is vital. So is cashflow and these days the need to chase is, perhaps regrettably, the norm.

- **selling-on,** as future contact is made, as a relationship is forged we want the contractual side to become easier. Next time the procedure is "as before", and if all went well this will be seen by the customer as reasonable, straightforward and hassle-free.

This is an important area to deal with effectively, it is an integral part of many sales processes. If delayed, skimped or ignored it will certainly cause problems. Contracts and terms are, after all, primarily for when things go wrong, it is only then that many need to turn to the "letter of the law". Get this area right and it provides a firm basis for profitable business.

57. Do not sound egocentric

Selling inevitably involves an egocentric approach. You have to think of it as your meeting, you want — indeed intend — it to be successful, you have to go for the objective, and that is always ultimately to close and this could be stated as getting your own way. All true and necessary, yet this approach should not show inappropriately and must now show overtly in your language.

So, do not prefix things you say by, for example: "If you want my opinion . . . ", or "If I were you I would . . . ". It too easily sounds patronising. Customers may well be interested in your advice, but they expect it to be tailored to them, and based on consideration of their circumstances. Much better to lead into comments with something like: "For a company of your size the best approach is often . . . ", or "Given what you said about delivery, we might best deal with it like . . . "

Customers want to know, and to recognise clearly, that you are acting on their behalf and that what you say has their interests in mind; your opinion in isolation they can do without. You will find a conscious line of avoiding egocentric sounding phraseology gives the customer the best impression, and helps position you as a professional.

58. Always be loyal to your company

You will sell more easily if your customers have not only a good relationship with you, but also a good image of the whole organisation you represent. Many firms spend a great deal of money creating a good background image through public relations, design and other techniques. Many sales people seem content to undo this good work in a moment. Consider the sales person faced with a complaint from a major customer because of late delivery. It is not his fault, the delivery instructions were clear, but a mistake has been made in the dispatch department and the customer, relying on the arrangement, is understandably upset. The salesman is concerned to protect his personal image and reputation and we can imagine him saying something along the lines of: "You will appreciate it was out of my hands, I don't know how many times I have told Distribution how important it is to meet customers' exact delivery instructions, but they still seem to get it wrong . . .". If he completes the sentence with the words "far too often" the damage is made worse, and in either case the customer is left feeling that however good the salesman, the organisation behind him is less than efficient. What may have been intended to bolster the salesman's image, ends up doing the reverse.

You may need to support company policy (even when you disapprove of it), defend colleagues who are less efficient than yourself and positively work at building the image of the whole company. The customer may well understand that no organisation is perfect, but one that seems to hold itself in low regard is seen as dubious – "If that is all they think of themselves" the customer thinks, "how can I have confidence in what they will do for me?" It is easy to let the wrong kind of description slip through, and if it becomes a habit, then the damage may be considerable. Boost the image of the whole of the organisation at every opportunity, even when you have to sort out difficulties, it can smooth the path for what follows and make what you do in selling just a little more certain.

59. Offer more

The advice in this book consists of matters sales people have the power to implement. So let me admit at once that this one may be dependent on company policy; yet it is an important and powerful aid to increasing sales so deserves a mention. You can increase sales by offering more; more than usual, more than competition, more than expected. Not just in terms of service – that point is made elsewhere – but in terms of tangible things. Many of the ways that spring to mind are temporary (they have less impact once they are permanent and taken for granted) and might be best described as promotional. For example, offer:

- a free sample or trial of the product or service
- a free element of product (eg. 12 for the price of 10)
- a limited or exclusive offer
- a saving, avoiding a coming price increase, an additional one-off discount, etc.
- a higher specification for the cost of the basic product
- an incentive (a gift, a trip, a competition)
- trade in allowances for upgrading product
- better than usual credit terms
- free or discounted spares or accessories
- special guarantees, or buy back arrangements
- staff training schemes
- discounts linked to future purchase

Any of these and more can increase sales. Such devices act in a number of different ways:

- they help you get a hearing, perhaps for the first time
- they help improve the weight of the case you can present
- they can pull orders forward, persuading people to order now rather than later
- they can increase the size of an order

- they can affect the frequency of ordering

They can also have negative effects, reducing the seeming importance of the actual product benefits, or encouraging customers to shop around and buy in turn from whoever is currently offering the best deal. They have to form an organised part of your company marketing strategy as they can affect image and profitability and cash flow. Some you may control, others you may find suggested and made available by management, perhaps on a temporary basis. Some you may feel would work well and suit your kind of customer, in which case you may want to suggest them to management.

Such schemes are undeniably useful, but you should never rely on them to the exclusion of making a sound case for buying in other ways.

Handling Objections

Objections are an inherent part of selling. They spring direct-ly from the way customers look at the situation and you can be sure there will always be some. Your prospects raising them is not necessarily a sign that there is any problem, indeed it can be a sign of some interest on their part. So han-dling objections is an inherent part of the sales job. If this part is done well it does not only redress the balance, or remove the objection entirely, its being well handled will be impres-sive. Customers like dealing with a salesman who as they might put it: "knows their stuff". The smooth handling of objections is taken as a sign of professionalism. Not that you will always be able to remove them, there is no merit in try-ing to persuade your customers that black is white and the last thing you want is an argument. Rebalancing is what counts as the points below investigate.

60. Taking the positive view

Some say objections are a sign of interest. This makes sense, cus-tomers will not bother quizzing us about the details and expla-nations of something that interests them not at all. Certainly you should expect them. The way customers go about making buy-ing decisions is to weigh up the pros and cons, they expect to find some things on the downside (few things we buy are per-fect, they may be suspicious if it is!). You should watch, howev-er, for the quantity of objections you get. Too many can be a sign that it is your fault. By this I mean that with experience you will know roughly how much objection will be raised, and to some extent on what issues. If you find that a kind of customer in a kind of meeting you run regularly is raising more than you expect, then it may be that:

- you have failed to identify his needs sufficiently accurately and what you are saying is therefore off target. More questions may correct this
- you are suggesting solutions or making suggestions too soon. Customers who feel their situation is unique or who expect a tailored recommendation may feel that should follow more thought
- you may be giving the impression of a set, standard presentation. Customers disbelieve that products can be all things to all people, they want you to relate what you sell to them individually, not simply go through the standard "patter".

In all these cases observation may spot what is happening and allow you to adjust your approach.

So, objections can help keep you on track, they are a sign of interest and can also be an opportunity to impress customers by the way you deal with things (not that you should encourage objections just so that you can impressively demolish them!). When they do occur however, and they will, there is no reason why you cannot regard them as something routine and something that you can use to build your credibility as you go along.

61. Preventing objections

It is a sound principle in many areas that prevention is better than cure. In objection handling there are two ways in which prevention can help. The first is in the area of preparation. Few objections should come at you like a bolt from the blue, most of the topics of objection that occur you will know about and have dealt with previously. You should have thought through the perennial objections and, although they will often be phrased in different ways and come with different power and emphasis, you should be ready for them with various ways of handling them in mind. As and when new, or differently phrased, objections do occur then you need to think about possible answers to these too and add something about them to your repertoire.

Secondly, there are objections that may typically remain unspoken. This does not mean they are not in customers' minds, some will be and will form part of the balance upon which they will ultimately decide to buy or not. Where experience shows that this is likely to be happening it may be necessary to raise the issue yourself in the conversation in order to deal with it and get it out of the frame. This is best approached head on: "You have been wondering about . . . let me spend a minute explaining how we deal with that . . . "You have not mentioned . . . do you have any questions about that?". And if you have thought through the answer, or at least the kind of answer, necessary then you can deal with the matter and perhaps also make it seem reasonably inconsequential.

62. "Sparring" with objections

We do not demolish objections, we are not even always able to overcome them and we certainly do not want objection handling to develop into an argument. Indeed it is quite possible to win arguments with customers — yet lose the order. If, when the customer raises an objection, your hackles immediately rise and your every response chips in starting with the words "Ah, but . . . ", there is every chance that the conversation will become confrontational. It is for this reason that you should use the technique known as "sparring". Sparring concerns offering an appropriate initial response, and is useful preliminary to the process of objection handling. The sparring needs to make clear:

- that you are listening carefully
- that there will be no argument
- that you accept the point made and will deal with it rather than deny it
- that you will treat it seriously
- that you do not think the customer is being contentious, or unnecessarily demanding.

If you say something that positions how you will deal with the objection: "That's a good point, Mr Customer, I can see I must give you more information in that area . . .", "You are quite right to raise that, it is an important point, let me . . . ", preferably something that includes at least a hint of agreement, then you will provoke feelings in the customer's mind that will make dealing with the objection easier. With the customer saying to himself: "Good, there's not going to be an argument" or "He accepts the point, let's see what he says about it" then he is receptive to what you say next. This principle may be more important than it seems because some objection areas are difficult and can quickly become emotional. Sparring has the effect of "lowering the temperature" of the conversation prior to providing an answer.

There is another important result of using this technique. Sometimes you will get objections that are new, that you are not expecting, not familiar with or that throw you, presenting real difficulty when you feel you have to come back fast with a credible response. Luckily the construction of the human mind is such that in the time it will take you to say something like: "That's good point, Mr Customer, we are certainly going to have to satisfy you that we can meet your needs in that area. Let me . . .", then your mind can be doing a great deal of thinking. Sparring builds in a bit of time to think just when you may need it most; very useful that can be too. It sets up a situation that is as favourable as possible to dealing with the objection itself, and makes it more likely that you can do so effectively.

63. Providing an answer

Never attempt to deal with an objection until you have sufficient information. If you assume wrongly exactly what is meant or treat a serious point superficially you will be in trouble and make matters worse. Objections must not be allowed to put you on the defensive. Sparring helps set the scene. Two other initial responses are also well worth bearing in mind. First, never be afraid to respond to a question with a question. This will be understood and accepted, after all how can you be expected to comment sensibly about a point until you know exactly what lies behind it? More than one question may be quite acceptable, though you should make it clear what you are doing: "That's a fair point, Mr Customer, let me make sure I understand exactly what you mean, can you tell me . . . ". This is an important point as simple questions or comments may either disguise a deeper point or, more often, have many interpretations. Consider an example. A customer comments on price (they so often do!) saying something like: "But that is very expensive". What do they mean? It is a comment, not even phrased as a question and could mean many things, for instance it could mean:

- "It is more than I expected"

- "It is more than I pay now"
- "It is more than another quote"
- "It is over my budget"
- "That cost is beyond my authority to decide"
- "I'm not convinced it is value for money"
- "Will you negotiate?"
- "I'm not clear what I get for it"
- "It is a lot to pay at once"
- "I don't understand"
- "No"
- "Can the product specification be reduced to cut costs?"
- "I will have to think about that"
- "I cannot decide now"

You may well be able to think of, or have experienced, more. Clearly many of these interpretations need answering along different lines; it makes the point clearly that you have to understand exactly what is meant before you deal with it.

Secondly, if something is thrown out as a comment or challenge, just like "But that is very expensive" in the above example, in a form that is not a question, then it may be turned back to the customer as a question in order to clarify. Thus "But that is very expensive" could be followed by the question: "Yes, Mr Customer, it is a considerable cost, though I would suggest, of course, it is a good investment, but what exactly are you saying? Is it more than you had budgeted for?" This kind of approach does a number of things quickly, it acknowledges the point (there is no merit in denying it is a great deal of money if he clearly feels it is) suggests you will be happy to discuss it and makes asking for more information about his concern seem helpful.

Once these preliminaries are out of the way, you can move on to actually address the objection. If you continue to keep in mind the image of a balance (see page 55) and bear in mind that there will be points — of varying importance, weight, on either side — then the job is one of ordering the balance, or reordering the one you have described, so that it presents a favourable basis for a positive decision. Often, of course, customers are not going to automatically buy if the balance is positive, they are only going to buy from you if your described balance stacks up better than those of any competitors which they may also be evaluating.

You have three options in rebalancing. One, you persuade them the objection is false, in other words it exerts no weight on the minus side of the balance. Two, you concede they have a point, but explain that the effect on the balance is minimal. Or three, you have to concede completely and in this case – and the others – combine within your answer a re-emphasis on the plus points, that is the benefits.

Careful description of price will minimise the incidence of price objections, careful handling of them will remove what can often be a major obstacle to sales.

64. Handling price

Of all the things that come up as objections this is often the most frequent and the most difficult. Of course, all customers want value for money, and in many areas they will negotiate if they can (negotiation is an additional skill to that of selling, beyond the scope of this book. If you are interested in it, my earlier book for Kogan Page *Agreed!* covers this topic, as do other books in the Kogan Page business list). At the least they want to assess value for money and often to compare what you offer in this respect with competition. So how do you handle this? First, the way you position price has an effect on the likelihood of your subsequently receiving price objections. Price should rarely be dealt with alone, by describing it with benefits then you make it speak much more of value for money.

Beware also presenting price so that it runs foul of the way in which people regard money psychologically. For example:

- *avoid price barriers:* something priced at £9.99 is perceived as being significantly less than something at £10, similarly with higher amounts, £4995 seems less than £5000. This seems silly to many, we know it is virtually the same thing, but there is a great deal of research to back this up. I suggest you do not worry about why, but use the fact where you can.
- *amortise price:* this is the technique of quoting a figure of, say, £1000 (or around a thousand) per month, which seems less than £12,000 over a year. This can be used in a variety of ways to split larger sums down, spreading them over differ-ent budgets, people, time frames, etc.

If you have more flexibility in setting prices, as is the case with those selling a tailored service, for example, then:

- **judge price range carefully**: to say it will be between £4000 and £7000 may seem too vague, whereas £4000 — £5000 or even £5500 may be acceptable as a first ballpark figure. A second point here, always be careful about the top point of the range. Quote something you then exceed and the customer's perception of you changes for the worse and does so at once: "These people always go over their estimate" — come in below estimate and it helps ensure they come back to you next time.
- **avoid round figures:** when quoting bespoke arrangements, if you are tailoring a system say, and the work is based on the customer's unique brief, it will not come to a figure like £10,000. They will think this an impossible coincidence and probably assume that you have worked it out and rounded it up.

Finally here, a useful way to remember some good phraseology when dealing with price can be hung round the four mathematical symbols:

+ mention: this **plus** . . ./in **addition to** . . .
− mention: . . . **reducing** costs/**eliminating** the need for . . /**lessening** this . . ./**minimise** . . .
× mention: . . . something producing **multiple** advantages or opportunities/**enhanced** service/. . . **greater** productivity/**more** satisfaction
− mention: **amortise** costs over . . ./**spread** across . . ./**divided** between . . ./**apportioned** to . . .

65. Dealing with the ups and downs of price

Price is always an issue and when it changes this can focus more attention on it. Most usually the problem of changes is with increases, but sometimes there are, perhaps curiously, also problems with reductions in price. We will review reduction first.

Sometimes the company can reduce price (not by negotiating, but as a marketing tactic), this may be linked to technological changes — or to competitive pressure; there are many reasons. Unsolicited gifts can arouse suspicion, and if customers are told "Prices are down by 10%", their first reaction may not be "Good", but "Why?". Reactions include:

- **replacement:** it is assumed that a line is being discontinued, that it has become obsolete and will be replaced by some- thing better or more up to date. Here reasons are vital, you need to offer reassurance of quality and say what makes the reduction possible.
- **trouble**: it is assumed that the company is in trouble, usually financial trouble, and that a rapid cut is designed to produce cash that will assist the process of recovery. Here you need to boost their overall image of the company, talk about long term plans and make clear that things are going well.
- **low quality**: customers assume that the product under offer is of low quality and perhaps different from the rest of the range or from what they are used to receiving from you. Talk about quality control, tests and checks. Tell them how any rejects are in fact disposed of and reassure them regarding the specific offer.
- **bigger savings**: a cut may be taken, perhaps in conjunction with one of the other factors, to mean greater cuts are to fol- low. This can also result in no order now and you need to make it clear if this is not the case. If the cut is for a short time this can be quoted, if there are regular dates for future change remind them of this.

On the other hand, and maybe with greater regularity, prices may be increased and you need to discuss this with customers who regard it as unreasonable. In this case:

- **explain the reasons**: and there should be reasons! Cost increases, economic situations — better still link it to the cus- tomer's own situation, when did they last raise prices and why?
- **help them reduce the impact**: this can be done by suggesting larger orders (if quantity rates apply); early ordering (even one more order at the old price may soften the blow); suggest ways to save associated costs (delivery charges, packaging, installation or maintenance)

Everyone knows products and services cost money and that prices change sometimes. Make the explanation clear and what- ever the change you can keep the customer on your side, con- tinue to retain his business and even sell more than before.

66. Do not knock competition

Sometimes you will be asked outright about competition: "What about firm X?" Or "We also plan to talk to company Y, do you know them?" Two responses are to be avoided. First, do not single them out: "Yes, I know them, they are my biggest competitor". Such a response is likely to make the buyer think he should check them out, indeed you may end up with one more active competitor vieing for the business. Secondly, do not knock them: "Know them, I thought everyone knew the trouble they are having in the market at present". It is just life that at that point that they declare that they have done business together very satisfactorily in the past, or that there is some other connection that makes a knock particularly inappropriate. Besides, it is very difficult not to let such comments sound like sour grapes. You need a more constructive response, something like: "There are a dozen or more competitors for us in this sector, we come across them all and each has certain strengths". This makes checking them all out seem complicated, and while giving no detail, does acknowledge that you know they are also good. Such is also a more credible response.

Another, perhaps similar thing, that can happen is that customers refer to the competition's comments about you: "Your competitors tell me you are having delivery problems with the 646 model at present, is that right?" This kind of comment can be turned round: "If my rivals are making a point of saying that kind of thing, then my first reaction is only to be pleased. It seems to me to indicate we have them worried in that product area — the 646 is certainly proving very popular, and production has been raised to cope with this, you will find delivery is now just as good as on the rest of the range".

Care in all references to competition always pays off, the last thing you want is a protracted argument prompted by some detailed negative comment the customer then feels he must defend as accepting it may make his past decision to deal with another firm look ill judged. One last point, if a competitor is named (and it is something you can do worse than ask about if not) then information about what you are up against may well help you decide on the line you will take with the customer; provided you know something about your competitor's strengths and weaknesses that is.

67. Avoid untenable comparisons

There is an old saying to the effect that while you can compare apples with apples, there is no merit in comparing apples with old shoes. Yet customers do the latter all the time. They say something like: "That's all very well but I can get the same thing from Firm X on much better terms". What they actually mean is that they can get something rather different from elsewhere. On that basis they are no doubt correct, there are always many permutations on offer in any particular industry. They seek justification of your package, and very often of price (they may want a discount), in comparison with the quoted alternative — though they rarely elaborate on the details of that other offering.

The answer cannot lie with a direct comparison when, as is most often the case, the two things are not exactly the same. A quoted competitor may be less costly, but the specification may be less, the quality lower, less may be included, service or running costs may be higher, credit terms or guarantees may be different, design details may vary, delivery may be longer or less certain. The possibilities are many.

A sales response must identify and then deal with these differences. The first answer may well be "Yes, you can buy something similar elsewhere" (do not deny it, that way lies fruitless argument) "but it is certainly not identical, in our discussions you have emphasised the need for reliability, our . . . " and back to the benefits you have identified they want. In some circumstances the first response may need to be a question; you have to find out more about what is being offered to discover how in fact it differs from your offering. In terms of price, if yours are more expensive then the additional amount over and above your competitor can only be explained and justified by reference to the gap between what the two parties offer, in other words what does the extra amount of money buy? — better service, higher productivity or what? Or indeed what would paying less lead them to miss, for you can discuss it both ways round.

Customers want value for money, they also want a "good deal", but they will not sacrifice key requirements for savings which may prove a false economy. It is a fact that many of the most successful products and services in many markets are not the cheapest. Cost and quality go together and you should sell your quality with confidence. Avoid odious comparisons which customers may make only to antagonise, or as an opening to negotiation, and make sure that whatever the customer may do, you only compare apples with apples.

68. Use the "boomerang" technique

This is a form of words which turns an objection back on itself so that the question posed links to the answer. Thus:

- "As you know this is now very urgent, I don't know that we have time for elaborate tests"
- *"It is because I know you want things up and running fast, Mr Customer, that I am suggesting the test. It will not take long and could avoid more significant delays if you went ahead without and hit any snags"*

If the question is linked to something that the customer rates highly, and if he needs the products urgently, then this can work well. Though it will sound contrived unless you really can make a case for the line you present. It is a manner of presentation which can make the customer feel that his key issue is genuinely being acknowledged and that the answer is being dealt with in a way which addresses it.

69. Saving face

Sometimes the customer's objections prove false. This makes him challenge some point when in fact the facts are entirely on his side and the balance is good and positive. The temptation in a hectic meeting, especially one in which a fair number of objections have been raised, including perhaps some difficult ones, is heave a sigh of relief that one is mistaken and blurt out the equivalent of "You're wrong!" This is a natural reaction but can result in the customer being made to feel bad, or worse, feeling he has been made to look silly. Clearly this is something to be avoided if good relations are to be maintained.

There can be many reasons for the customers making a mistake, his original impression about the company or its product or service may be wrong, out-of-date perhaps. He may have misheard something or misinterpreted something he read, or it could be your fault — you may have put something badly, not gone into sufficient detail, gone on talking while his attention was elsewhere; you may not know where the fault lies, indeed it may not matter.

What is important is to let the customer down lightly. Suggest it is an easy or commonly-made mistake. This may still leave him feeling bad. It may be better than this to suggest you are at fault, albeit in a general and unspecified way: "Sorry, perhaps I gave you the wrong impression about that, the fact is . . .", "If I was insufficiently clear about that, I apologise, it is not, in fact, a problem; the fact is . . . ". This works well in either case. Sometimes the customer knows he is at fault and rather likes an approach that avoids laying blame or making him feel bad about it. Sometimes it is no one's fault but the approach is still seen to be sensitive. Just a little care in this area can get over what otherwise can be small upsets to the smooth progress of the meeting and the development of a positive case. You should not overdo it, or it will risk sounding patronising, but to avoid drawing attention to errors.

Gaining A Commitment

It is the need to close that sets selling — persuasive communication — apart from other more straightforward kinds of communication. It can involve getting the other person to make a decision, change their minds or even upturn the habits of a lifetime. As such it can present problems. It is psychologically difficult in some senses for the salesman, holding out as it does the prospect of success, or failure. And customers sometimes find it difficult to make a decision. It is a stage that is dependent on what has gone before, but one that must occur. If you cannot or will not close and handle that stage well then your sales effectiveness will always be less effective than it might otherwise be. Here we review this crucial stage.

70. Your own commitment to close

Closing a deal is the ultimate objective of all selling. You can reach it in stages, in which case you have to close, a number of times, on all the interim commitments of which there can be many, it may represent a close to get a customer to say:

- yes, I'll see you
- yes, send samples (or literature)
- yes, let me have a quotation in writing (or a proposal)
- yes, let's meet again to take things further
  and, of course ultimately, yes, I'll buy it.

Closing is less a stage of the sales process, than just a phrase or, more often, a question. You have to know when to close and you have to do it. Closing is often a weak area of selling and that may be less because it is done badly, than because it is not done at all. Sales people, who understandably dislike it when people say "No" (and not all prospects say no politely), may find themselves taking a safer route to ending the meeting. They say things like: "I hope this has been useful", "I hope I have been able to give you all the details you need at this stage", "Is there anything else I can add before we finish?" This kind of non-close finish almost guarantees a pleasant end to the meeting with customers responding with statements such as: "That's been very useful, thanks very much for coming to see me", "You've given me all the information I need at this stage, thank you very much for your time". All very nice, everyone likes to feel they have been helpful and everyone likes to receive thanks; but such responses are usually followed by two other little words: "Good Bye" drawing the meeting to a close before a commitment has been made and before any follow-up action can be arranged.

So resolve to close. You have to be thick-skinned about the rejection; I do not know an area of selling with a one hundred per cent strike rate, so there is always some. But if you aim to close every time at every stage then, along with a little rejection, you may well get more business than any of your more faint hearted competitors.

71. Watch for buying signals

The advice is often given that the best time to close is at the earliest time possible. This is a little glib, but there is some truth in it, to the extent that you can leave things too late and the moment passes. Certainly you need to watch for signs that the prospect is ready to make a decision. Left alone some buyers are very indecisive, or at the least they will take a long time to make up their minds. This may be for constructive reasons — you must be wary of trying to shortcut the buyer's weighing up factors which he sees as making a decision possible — but if it is just out of what some salesmen might see as a perverse desire to delay, then closing may act as a catalyst to prompt a decision.

Remember closing does not cause people to buy, only the power of persuasion from the picture you have built up and the case you have put over can do that — by creating the interest that closing then converts into becoming a decision to buy. So the final kind of feedback you need during a sales meeting is in the form of what are called "buying signals". These are less easy to define than to spot. Some will be in the form of a series of signs of interest, expressions, comments, noises even, nods certainly, all of which indicate satisfaction with what is being presented. The most tangible sign is probably comments about situations after purchase, for example: "Then after we have the system installed we can . . .", "Once this stage is out the way we . . . ". Such comments may well be interspersed with questions and other signs that some portion of the decision is still to be made, finally the questions may only be for reassurance; in his own mind he has made the decision – and closing can confirm it out in the open.

You will come to trust your judgment in this area and it is well worth while noting what signals you feel you see, and whether they provide an accurate indication of how things went from there on.

72. Obtaining feedback from the trial close

It is important to realise that closing is not a one-shot situation, some sales meetings involve a number of closes, the first rejected but the last agreed. One early close that may be used to obtain feedback – with no real hope of actually closing at the point it is used is the so called "trial close". This can really be any kind of close in terms of technique: you may be pretty sure the answer will be a no, but the way it is phrased can give valuable clues to how close you are getting to acceptance or on what element you should now concentrate. For example, if you attempt to close, the customer might say: "Now wait a minute, we still need to discuss payment terms", and you move on to discuss just that. This is a useful technique and provides an alternative way of obtaining very focussed feedback.

73. How to close

Closing is not a stage but more a simple question or comment. All you need is a particular choice of phraseology to match the customer and the circumstances. There are many permutations, but the most often used are perhaps the following:

Direct request
For example, "Shall we go ahead then, so that you start getting these financial savings soon?"

Requests like this should be used where the customer likes to make his own decisions.

Command
For example, "Install this new system in each regional office. It will give you the information you want much more quickly and help you to make more effective decisions."

This can be used where the customer:

- has difficulty in making a decision; or
- has considerable respect for the sales person.

Immediate gain
For example, "You mentioned that this year the company really needs to improve productivity. If you can give me the go-ahead today, I can make sure that you see specific results within three months' time."

This could be used where, by acting fast, the customer can get an important benefit, whereas delay might cause him severe problems. The "hard" version of this is the . . .

Fear close
As in "Unless you can give me the go ahead now, then . . .". This is a more powerfully phrased version of "immediate gain", and should be used with discretion.

Alternatives
For example, "Both these approaches meet your criteria. Which one do you prefer to implement?"

This could be used where the sales person is happy to get a commitment on any one of the possible alternatives.

'Best solution'
For example, "You want a system that can cope with flexible demands, that is easy for staff to operate without training and is presented in a form that will encourage line managers to use it. The best fit with all these requirements is our system 'X'. When's the best time to install it?"

This should be used when the customer has a mix of needs, some of which can be better met by the competition, but which, when taken as a whole, are best met by your solution.

Question or objection
For example, "If we can make that revision, can you get the finance director to agree to proceed?"

This should be used where you know you can answer the customer's objection to his satisfaction.

Assumption
For example, "Fine. I've got all the information I need to meet your requirements. Once I get back to the office I'll prepare the necessary paperwork and you'll have delivery by the end of the month."

In other words, we assume the customer has said "Yes" and continue the conversation on this basis.

Concession
Trade only a small concession to get agreement now or agree to proceed only on stage one.

However you phrase the question, the key thing here is to actually close and do so firmly; more than once if necessary and with every customer at every stage of the process.

74. Responding to the customer who says "Let me think about it"

Customers may say a number of things other than "Yes" or "No", and many find the most difficult to deal with is that little phrase "Let me think about it". This is essentially positive, yet if you walk away from it then you may never speak to that customer again. Some customers who say this actually mean "No". You need to know whether to take it at face value or not. So what is the best response? It is often very difficult to think of a reason why the customer should not think about it (unless perhaps you can contribute pressing reasons to decide at once). So the best route may well be to agree. And not simply to agree but to urge the customer to think about it. Tell him it is an important decision, tell him he must not make it lightly, tell him he should not be rushed, that he must be certain; however you phrase it make sure you are clearly on the side of thinking about it. But then ask why he still needs to think about it, or what elements of the decision still need review. Often something is volunteered here, there is a particular sticking point, something about the case has been less well made than the rest, or there is some area where more information seems to be needed. Then you can try turning the intention back to more discussion:

- "Let me think about it"
- "*Of course, it's a big decision, you have to be sure*"
- "That's right"
- "*You must be sure it's right in every respect, is there any particular aspect which you need to think about particularly?*"
- "Well, I suppose it's the installation time that worries me most, its bound to affect current work"
- "*To some extent yes, but we can overcome that, perhaps I did not explain how we would approach that sufficiently; can I go over it again before we finish?*"
- "O.K. I want to have it all clear in my mind"

The meeting is under way again now and there is no reason why it cannot move towards another close (Final Objection close can be right in this sort of situation) which is agreed without any more wish to think about it. The phrase is regularly a sign that something, and it may be several somethings — in which case you may be able to get the customer to list them before you suggest more discussion — is still unclear or unresolved.

There is an alternative here, however. The customer may ask for time to think about it not because they need time to think, but for some other reason. Perhaps the two most likely are the need to confer with someone else in the organisation (the real decision maker?), or maybe there is a competitor around and a meeting planned with them for comparative purposes. Either possibility, or others, may be discovered by careful questioning. In which case the action on which you plan to close may change; maybe the first step is to try to organise a meeting with their colleague (sometimes they appreciate help with any internal selling that may be necessary), or to ensure you get a further hearing after the competitor meeting. Again we see that the better the information you find out at every stage, the better position you are in to take things further. Such techniques are not infallible, but if they increase your strike rate even a little they are well worth pursuing.

75. When they say "Yes"

Let us assume you are going to achieve a good strike rate — think positive! — some of the buyers you see will agree to buy. Then what? Well, the first thing is to thank them, you do not need to grovel, but the nature of the relationship makes a thank you highly appropriate. It is good practice to couple the thanks with reassurance: "Thanks very much, Mr Customer, I am sure you will find it works well". Then consider any practical points that need to be dealt with at this stage:

- do you need a signature?
- is there documentation to be completed (guarantee, contract, service arrangement, etc)?
- is there information you need (invoice address, order number, delivery arrangements, etc)?
- are there points still to be discussed/agreed (delivery date)?

All such matters must be dealt with in a prompt and business-like way, you are still on show and it is still possible for the customer to change his mind, or demand to negotiate more on price — something that will negate the result you think you have achieved. So deal with such things promptly and end the meeting. Do not chatter on in a fit of euphoria, many a salesman has talked himself out of the order again at that stage. Of course some social chat may be important, there are deals where lunch afterwards is regarded as natural by both parties. Just be a little careful, be sure the customer — who no doubt values his time highly — really wants to extend the contact. And decide the objectives of such an extended meeting. Do you drop business, talk no "shop" and treat it socially, or use it to move on to other topics? It is important to meet the customer's needs in this respect. He will not like it if he planned to use the time constructively and you just talk golf or vice versa.

Once you have left the customer, never fail to double check your internal paperwork is completed. Salesmen have been known to forget something as vital as the quantity ordered after a good dinner!

Reinforcing Your Case

The techniques that can help build your case, strengthen it and make it more likely to prove one that will be agreed, are, as we have already seen, many and various. There are factors that can have potentially powerful effects on what you do that do not fall exclusively into a neat category. Here we review some of these additional factors.

76. Use your colleagues in joint calling

Not even the best sales person can do everything. The complexities of most business and many customers mean that some situations inevitably need the skills, expertise and experience only available through a combination of people working together. This is a fact of business life, it should not be regarded as a sign of weakness and avoided but used where appropriate to secure sales that might be unachievable any other way.

So who do you work with? There are a number of options: a colleague, another sales person with different experience or skills, a member of technical support or service, staff from research or a member of the management team — including your sales manager. The key to making joint calls work is planning and, if necessary, rehearsing. You must think about and agree who will do what and who, above all, will be in the chair, directing the meeting and bringing the other in as appropriate. Whose call is it to be in other words.

Never go out to a customer in a team without sitting down and talking through how you will handle the meeting. Decide who will introduce who and how. You need to be clear how you will explain to the customer the need for two of you, or more, to be there. If one of you knows the buyer, introduce the newcomer, always making it clear that something about his experience or expertise makes his contribution valuable to the customer. Never give the impression that things are being handed over to someone less important or less qualified to assist than the prime contact. A suggested agenda for such a meeting may be very useful to help keep it organised. Do not give the impression of crowding or pressurising the customer by arriving "mob-handed", the reason needs to be stated in customer terms: "So that we can go through some of the technical detail and take things further without delay I have brought along my colleague . . . who will . . .".

If you have worked out in advance how you will handle things, the meeting can be as effective as any other, and, in fact may be more so, or at least allow good additional factors to be brought in to play. Good teamwork is always impressive. The customer will draw conclusions about how the company works and your likely service and quality from his observation of how you go about things. Hence the importance of preparation and rehearsal. The meeting must be "seamless", that is handover from one person to another on your side must be smooth and without hesitation. You cannot afford to say things like: "I think that's all on that, now John you were going to deal with service matters weren't you?" What you do between you must appear fluid and certain and must end by giving the customer all he wants as certainly as any other meeting.

Consider also small advantages of working together. One may be the designated note taker, freeing the other to concentrate on the conversation. One may be able to think through some problem while a colleague is talking and so resolve a point quickly and impressively on the spot. While you should not now suddenly resolve never to go to a meeting on your own again, do consider those few key meetings that can benefit from this approach and use them carefully — they can sometimes produce disproportionate sales results.

77. Develop a fluency with figures

I once saw a buyer running rings round a salesman with whom he was negotiating. The buyer kept tapping away at a large desk top calculator and then quoting figures to find fault with the salesman's argument. It sounded very authoritative and the salesman took the figures as gospel and, because his cost-effectiveness argument seemed flawed, agreed to a larger discount than he had originally intended. Yet the buyer did not have the calculator plugged in, the figures he was quoting were pure bluff; but he still achieved his objective.

Few sales people will admit to being weak at finance, but they are simply not sufficiently numerate to cope sufficiently quickly and certainly — with the sort of situation depicted above. If you are in this category, and feel any kind of vulnerability in this way, then you need to compensate.

How do you do this? More training may be necessary, but here let us make a simpler point. If there are any areas (the numbers may just be one) where your ability to project and deal with your case is weaker than you would like, then you must prepare what you do in those areas more thoroughly. Make a whole range of calculations before the meeting. Work out every kind of permutation you think may need dealing with. Turn things into more manageable form — using graphs is one useful way of making figures easier to follow. Use modern technology, maybe a programmable calculator can help. Make sure you are not lagging in this important area.

Business, and therefore selling, is about money. Accountants may deal with such issues seemingly without the need for thought (though someone once said that there are three kinds of accountant; those who can add up and those that cannot!). You do not need to be a qualified accountant to be successful at selling, but you do need a degree of numeracy that matches the needs of the work you do and in many businesses nothing less will do.

78. Be good on your feet

It is an international trend that more and more sales jobs are demanding that those that do them are not only good at presenting their case one to one, across the desk, but also on their feet in formal, stand up, presentations. The buyer may increasingly be the Board, the staff of a department, a committee or a group of some other sort. In some businesses they talk of the "beauty parade", and business does not come without passing over this necessary hurdle.

Presentation skills are not the stock in trade of everyone in selling and there is a great deal of difference between presenting sitting comfortably across the table from someone you know well and facing an apparently hostile or indifferent group of, say, a dozen people whose expectations are unclear. Hence the old saying: "The human brain is a wonderful thing — it starts working on the day you are born — goes on and on — and only stops on the day you have to speak in public". If you are not good at presenting and have to do it or may have to in the future, then it is a skill you must acquire. Not everyone will ever be a great orator, but nearly everyone can learn to make a reasonable presentation, and anyone's style will improve with a little thought.

The first rule is preparation. So is the second and the third. Think about what you want to say, think about what order you will say it in, think about how you will say it — from tone of voice to example, from visual aid to dramatic pause. And arrange it with the classic beginning, middle and end. Make notes not to read from (this is for most rather difficult) but to guide you. Practice, practice, practice. Once you are sure you are clear what you are going to do and how, it will be easier.

Make no mistake, a good presenter has an edge on the poor. People do not say "what a pity he is a poor presenter, but I am sure the product is good". They are more likely to say "That seems poor"; full stop. So it is an important skill and worth some separate study, as there are good many "tricks of the trade" to get your mind round. It is too big a topic to do justice to here (my book *Making Successful Presentations* (Sheldon) deals with it in detail). Add good presentation skills to your armoury and it will stand you in good stead for the future in career terms as well as in selling terms.

79. Use your authority

Customers need to see you as their prime contact with authority to deal with all aspects of their business with your organisation. This does not mean that you must be the only person from the company they ever meet. But it does mean you have to be careful to introduce others in a positive context. It is one thing to introduce someone to augement what you do, by providing a necessary higher level of technical information or expertise, for instance; it is quite another to seek help, advice or decision in a manner which indicates a clear gap in your authority.

As an example, consider the area of returns. In one company (they sold high priced publications – research reports and directories, etc) customers would sometimes find they had bought something that did not, in fact, give them the information they wanted; they would then seek a refund. Only the manager was able to make this decision as some customers were trying to pull a fast one, for example photocopying a few key pages and then seeking to save the money. So the sales person responded to such a request by saying "Please wait", and went to check with the manager. The manager's decision was rarely, if ever, different from that the sales staff would have made, but it was clear to the customer that the sales person did not have authority to make this decision. The customer read this as an opportunity to negotiate and instead of accepting, say, the opportunity to change for another publication, they wanted their money back or found some other problem to raise once the sales person returned.

As soon as a query is raised in any sales meeting, and the sales person says: "I must check that", "I will have to ask the manager", "It will need to be cleared with Head Office", the customer knows that the salesman lacks some authority and will often seek to take advantage of this fact. So it is helpful to ensure that you are able to deal with as much as possible that can occur with customers, to position yourself as the key contact and let them see you as the one who makes the decisions regarding their business. Any necessary checks, and there may well be some, can be made in the background, preferably before the meeting. Be seen to be in charge and your authority will be challenged less.

80. Make a point of not selling

It is said that modesty is the art of encouraging people to find out for themselves just how wonderful you are; in the same way not selling can sometimes persuade people to do business with you. Customers want and need to do business with and through salesmen, but they also want expert support from someone on the sales side they can trust. Too often they actually believe that this is the last thing they will get, that the sales person is only out for themselves and that if they shake hands with them they should count their fingers afterwards to check they are still all present. Sometimes, however, they find that they feel they really can trust the salesman. A number of things can be used to help them come more certainly to that conclusion: not being too "pushy" and exerting undue pressure, for instance.

Another method can be introduced with more positive intent. Literally saying that you are not selling. How do you do this? With phrases such as: "I believe honesty is always best, so let me tell you . . . "; "If I were a good salesman, I probably wouldn't tell you this, but let me say . . . ". Such phrases can also be linked to competition: "I know you are talking to X and I am pretty sure they will have promised . . . so and so . . ., I certainly wouldn't make any unrealistic guarantee, but what I can say is . . . ". You can even get the buyer focussing more on the sales techniques of your competitors than on what they say, by referring to their techniques specifically: "Now I know firm X have a clever answer to the objection you raise, but let me be honest, it is a problem, but we minimise it by . . . ". Next time he sees your rival he may well notice what he says on the topic and be inclined to be more suspicious of it than would otherwise have been the case.

Of course, such an approach must not be overused and must used carefully or it will certainly sound glib. But a regular feeling of this sort within your conversation can add the feeling to the conviction that you really do put satisfying your customers ahead of one more quick sale. Some will actually describe themselves like this: "I am glad I don't sell for X (a competitor), I am not nearly sales orientated enough. But my company put service to customers first, and if I take the same view there are many, like yourself, that seem to want that above all".

Take care with this approach, but remember there are many that will take some display of modesty as a sign that there is strength, expertise and other good qualities underneath — and who will dismiss any overt brashness as not to be trusted.

81. Consider swopping customers with your colleagues

No one sales person is going to be ideally suited to sell, equally successfully, to every one in the world. Sometimes customers will not respond because they will only do business if whoever is representing the company exhibits special skills or characteristics. As an example look at the number of companies who are recruiting Japanese, or Japanese speakers, to sell to the Japanese companies which are so evident in most parts of the world nowadays. Or it may be that special technical knowledge is necessary. Alternatively it may be that only a woman is acceptable as the sales person (as in selling cosmetics perhaps); or vice versa. Or that some buyers just do not like you. What a thought — surely everyone likes you? For most people, if they are honest, this is simply not true, none of us get on equally well with everyone and sometimes it is purely a matter of style or personality. Any factor may be incompatible; I once worked with a company where one customer said he would like to do business but would only do so if whoever came to talk to them was "longer in the tooth and shorter in the hair" than his first contact. He liked the product but, as a very traditional business with primarily older people at the senior levels, preferred to deal with someone older, less fashionable and more experienced. At least he said so, and business was obtained as a result. So be it, the customer is always right. Someone has to worry about allocating the right customer to the right member of the sales team.

If however you find this has not happened and you have apparently intractable problems with a particular prospect, then do consider swapping that prospect with one handled by one of your colleagues. This can sometimes break the deadlock. A new face may be seen in a different light. The customer who would not buy from you may then buy and you may get business from someone new. Refusing to recognise the problem will simply compound the problem, whereas a little informal networking around the sales team can pay dividends.

Follow-up and Persistence

Sales people are often described as being managers of their time, territory and customers. Certainly, as we have already seen, you are unlikely to succeed in selling without some measure of organisational skills. Selling is very much not just a case of handling the sales interview in the right way. Many sales are multi-stage, many things need following up, progressing from stage to stage until the customer has satisfactorily gone through the stages and processes they feel are necessary to making a decision. Successful salesmen recognise this fact and become adept at dealing with the follow up action required. Here we investigate these skills.

82. Handling a multi-stage contact

Not every sale is made by one visit or meeting, however well handled. In many businesses the process is multi-staged. This may take many forms. For example, a prospecting telephone call may lead to an appointment; at the meeting the prospect may indicate that another meeting, perhaps involving a colleague will be necessary in order to progress matters; at the second meeting the prospect agrees that what he is seeing looks good and is agreeable to the submission of a quotation (or in some industries a proposal); with the proposal submitted it may be necessary to arrange another meeting to tie things down, and this could take the form of a formal presentation to the Board or to a buying committee; after that maybe another meeting and . . . there could well be more. This sounds somewhat daunting, and indeed it can be, and the lead time involved can vary too, making for additional complications. From initial meeting to order may take days, weeks, months or many months, and a longer time may be no reflection on the way things have been conducted in the interim, it may be perfectly logical from the point of view of the client. As I write this I am reminded of some work I booked recently which took almost exactly two years to see through to that point; somewhat unusual in consultancy, but, like any order, welcome on the day confirmation finally came through.

However many stages there may be en route to an order and whatever they may be, it is clearly key that you progress the contact and steer it firmly from one stage to the next. Perhaps the longer the lead time, the greater is the need to do this systematically. The effect on the customer is sequential and cumulative. Unless each stage is effective and he is persuaded to take things further, the process may falter and no order will result. As time and effort must be put in to get from stage to stage, the further along the sequence things come to a halt, the greater the waste. The amount of time that is spent on follow up activity, making sure that you move firmly from one stage to the next, maintaining contact in the gaps, need not be great, even though the elapsed time may be many months. My two-year lead time mentioned above involved just two brief meetings and about ten telephone calls or letters while I tried to retain some patience and remain optimistic.

Without a doubt there is business that goes to those who are more systematic and persistent than their competitors. Being persistent is well worthwhile, but it is not altogether easy. Psychologically the calls that fill the gaps are awkward to make. What do you say when the prospect's secretary has told you three times in a week that "he is busy"? Well, you take it face value, at least to start with, and try to find out the best time to catch him. And you phone again. Sales people cannot afford to be paranoid, you need a thick skin and if you operate this way, making a firm date in your diary system so that you keep up the contact, then you will win more and lose touch with less.

83.   Use one contact to arrange the next

The closing objective at the end of every contact where on going contact is necessary is to arrange the next contact. You can either ask: "Can we get together again once you have those figures — when will that be?", or you can suggest: "Can I suggest we meet again once you have those figures — what about one day early next week?" Whatever the route the objective is to have specific agreement to a dated and timed further meeting (or whatever the next contact needs to be) before you walk out of the door or put down the telephone. You will not always succeed, but sometimes it will secure a commitment and that removes the need to follow up later which may be more awkward. If things are going well, if the customer has expressed an interest, agreed that you should submit a proposal, why not move on one more step and get them to agree the date of another meeting — all while they are in the mood to say yes.

84. Make good use of the telephone

A note of caution here. It is so easy to pick up the phone and make a call. Easier than ever when no meeting (or training course) seems complete without the occasional ringing of the now ubiquitous mobile telephone. But too often the dialling finger is put in gear before the brain; always ask yourself why you are phoning and make sure you have a reason — an objective you can state in customer terms. That said it is a convenient and useful way of keeping in touch.

The telephone is so much taken for granted that its correct use may well be forgotten. The following may seem basic, but it is important and getting matters absolutely right can increase a call's effectiveness. If you want to come over to the listener clearly then remember that the telephone exaggerates the rate of speech and hightens the tone. You must talk into the mouthpiece in a clear normal voice (if you are a woman it may help to pitch your voice lower than normal). It is surprising how many things can interfere with the simple process of talking directly into the mouthpiece: smoking, trying to write, or holding a file open for instance. There are other hazards to be avoided: a noisy office or a bad line. So remember:

- speak a little slower than in normal conversation
- it is said that if you smile it affects how you sound positively
- use a warm tone of voice
- put the emphasis on the key points
- be positive
- be concise, customers' time is valuable

- avoid jargon
- use gestures as you would face to face, it will change how you sound
- think about and project a clear, natural tone

Above all remember the customer *cannot see you*, obvious perhaps but it does mean your voice must do all the work. If you bear all these in mind the telephone will cease to be routine and will become a valuable element in the process of keeping in touch.

85. Drop them a line

Sales people often think of themselves as predominantly face-to-face people. They are more comfortable talking to customers than with other forms of communication and have a distaste for what they see as the chore of putting things in writing. Telephoning is the middle course, and undeniably provides a useful method of keeping in touch. But it is transient, in other words while it is a useful reminder of you and your products and company, it may well be quickly forgotten. A written message on the other hand is permanent, or at least potentially long lasting. It can therefore potentially have a greater effect. Besides it pays to ring the changes.

Not only is there a likelihood that you are less comfortable putting things into writing, but given the sales organisation of many companies, the typing resource is often not geared to salesmen who want to get out a quick note to a customer. Some have computers at home or use a portable and are able to originate text themselves. This may help, but some ability to get out neat typewritten material is important.

There are a number of ways and occasions when a letter is useful:

- to announce an intention to telephone (and perhaps to include the reason why)
- to announce a new product, proofs of a new advertisement, a new initiative, a new appointment (a short note and a copy of something such as a press release, giving the details may be appropriate here)
- to send something of interest to them (a press cutting, perhaps, or market intelligence that is beneficial to them)

- to invite them to something (a press function, an exhibition, a social function)
- and you can even get some value in terms of reminder from more mundane matters such as chasing an unpaid invoice, something that has to be done awkward though it may be: it is not a sale until the money is in the bank (and the cheque has cleared!).

You must judge the frequency carefully, something dropping through the post every five minutes like so much confetti will seem wasteful and may be regarded as exerting undue pressure. An occasional written reminder, especially if it in a form that is useful to the customer, works well.

86. Send a fax

Whatever did we do before we had the use of the fax? Few, if any, technical innovations have swept the business world so quickly and so completely and the speed and ease of contact they allow is invaluable. The very nature of the fax is different from other written communication, it has inherited the sense of urgency that was once the preserve of the cable and telex.

Fax also seems to have developed a certain informality. People write what are perhaps best described as external memos, with less of the formal headings and layout that characterises business correspondence. It is not uncommon to see handwritten external faxes, though usually only between people where some relationship has been built up; think carefully before you omit typing something, but there will be situations where you conclude rightly that it is not necessary.

All this adds options to what you can send to a customer, it makes matters such as confirming a meeting very straightforward. Do not overdo the urgency, remember that the quality at the receiving end is less than what you send — for some things a paper copy in the post makes sense — and, unless the customer's office has one of the newer plain paper copiers, fax is less permanent, fading over time, and less convenient.

Managing Customer Relationships

People do business, not organisations (though they may be the legal entity involved). Relations between the people who interface at the sales interview are very important. It is especially important when you hope the business will be ongoing, that regular business in fact will continue to come from a particular customer. This is something which you cannot rely on just happening, the next few heading review how you can make the likelihood more certain.

87. Create a role for yourself in your customers' businesses

Customers will do business with you on a regular basis if they value your product, approve your back-up service and more so if they respect and get on with you personally. But you can create a more powerful bond than this, you do not just want to be an occasional visitor, however pleasant they find you. You want to position yourself appropriately with regard to their business. Some of this positioning may involve peripheral elements to the real nature of your business. However if you can become regarded as, say, a valuable source of competitive intelligence as well as a professional representative, this will create a larger role for you.

Such a role can be stronger still. For example, many sales people have an advisory role inherent within their job, and this can go further than just a little competitive intelligence. One sales person I have dealt with regularly for some years has cultivated this kind of role very usefully. He sells print. I buy my business stationery, business cards and invoices from him. He also produces brochures I need for direct mail promotion of seminars and, where my client work involves print he may also be involved. His advice is excellent, whether it involves the additional cost of illustrations, how to choose sizes to avoid waste of paper in cutting, or explaining the differences between six different ways of varnishing a brochure to create exactly the right finish, he is helpful and his advice is sound. He will spend as much time over something on a speculative project for a client of mine, where he knows they will get a quote from a printer they already use and the chances of his getting the work are less, as he does on something much more certain. Because he gives freely of his time in this way and because his advice is good I would be reluctant to do any project involving print without having a word with him. More than this I feel some obligation to involve him on something new because of time he has spent in the past. The relationship makes sense both ways.

More to the point, it becomes very difficult for competition to break in on such a relationship. If you are more than a supplier, if you have a role in your customer's business, then the bond will be strong. It takes a while to work your way into such a position, but it is time well-spent. And it helps to think consciously about the kind of role you are seeking to fulfil and then work towards it. Like so much else in selling successfully, it does not just happen.

88. Control the "chat"

Of course selling can sometimes be more successful if you have good relationship with the customer and, while you do not have to like them all, some may well become real friends. Friendship may make some aspects of the sales process more difficult, as with closing, for instance. What is most important is that, like each other or not, there should be a professional respect between the two parties.

There is a story told of a salesman being asked to explain how he has managed to retain a customer for so long, regularly getting good business from him. He says it is all on account of the good relationship they have, that the customer is madly keen on golf and that as long as he checks how this is going, lets him recount how he won the weekend tournament, the relationship stays good and orders flow. When this same customer is asked why he does business with the salesman, he speaks highly of his professionalism, his technical expertise, his product knowledge and good service – but ends up by saying: "I just wish he would not go on so long about the golf!" There is a serious point here.

It is actually quite difficult to draw the line between taking an interest and getting on being a bore and wasting the customer's precious time. Good sales people draw this line very carefully and do not let their enthusiasm for a shared interest or any other distraction become – too time-consuming.

The moral is clear; be careful to balance the chatty elements of the conversation with the business elements. Too little informality and the relationship can be stifled to the detriment of doing business, too much chat and you will be seen as a time waster – in which case it will waste your time too and reduce your productivity.

89. Deliver!

This one word heading is not meant in the sense of getting the product delivered safely and on time. Rather it implies the personal delivery of elements of what the customer gets that are very much bound up in the person of whoever they deal with. By way of example, the following are key and make the point:

- Keep promises: always, always do what you say you will and do it by when you say you will. If you promise to get back to them by three o'clock with some figures, then you must do exactly that. And preferably do it before three. If you should find this will, in the event, not be possible then you must make contact before the deadline and rearrange – with an apology – an alternative arrangement. Better still always consider carefully the deadlines you set, it is better to give yourself a little more time and then better it, than be late. This may be especially true if the action you plan is dependent on others, in which case some contingency for their possible imperfections may be wise.
- Make your administration perfect: always ensure that documentation connected with your personal contact with a customer is right. This may be something simple you originate, like a letter to confirm an appointment. Or it may be more complex and originate elsewhere in your company. Make no mistake: if the guarantee, the service contract or the delivery note or the invoice is incorrect you are likely to be blamed. From the customer's point of view this is only logical, and it is no help to lay blame on others as they see you as fronting the

team. So details must be correct, everything must be in its place and, above all, it must all be clear and understandable.

Maintain a reputation of reliability with your customers and this can reinforce your position with them. Make them think not just twice but three or four times before they risk – and that is how you will make them see it, as risk – dealing with a competitor who they will fear may turn out not to deliver as you do. It is important before, during and after the sale. Brochures and quotations must be presented correctly, information prepared for and left with the customer at the end of a sales meeting, and follow up documentation and action of all sorts – all must deliver in exactly the way the customer wants.

Finally, it is worth remembering the old maxim that if you deliver a little more than promised, people notice, appreciate and remember.

90. Sort queries/complaints effectively

The concept of "delivering" explored above applies equally to dealing with difficulties. Before going any further it is worth stressing that there should not be many queries and complaints; things should be gotten right in the first place. Indeed, take time to get things right in the first place and you will not need to take time to get over the problem.

But let us be realistic, even the best run companies and the best sales people get a few negative things to sort out and when it does happen you can score points by responding fast, sorting it and getting the desired results quickly and certainly. This is true of simple queries. A figure is inappropriately omitted from a proposal and needs to be added. Done quickly, with an apology rather than an excuse, and with a good grace, then very little problem is caused.

If something more serious has arisen and a complaint is made, this must be picked up and handled well. A well chosen approach followed through logically is useful here as the natural human reactions (like saying it is not your fault, or starting to argue) can easily make things worse.

Though it is, hopefully, not something that occurs too often it is worth spelling out the principles involved. The following techniques should deal with the majority of complaints and action, whether on the telephone or face to face:

1. *Listen* to all the facts, reassure the complainant frequently with "Yes, I understand", and let him run out of steam. This gives time to think about what you will say, and what action to take. Write down the details and get his name, telephone number, etc. clearly, early on.

2. *Sympathise* and make him feel that you would feel the same way if you were in his shoes. Show him there will be no argument. Never interrupt with "But". Apologise, at least for his state of mind, and without necessarily taking the blame.

3. *Clarify* and make sure you have *all the facts right.* We should still keep away from arguing – the truth about the complaint may not be as it seems at first. Avoid "doubt" phrases such as "you claim" or "as I understand it", which make the customer feel he is being disbelieved; that will only make him reinforce his complaint.

4. *Summarise* his complaint, which will serve to check that you have all the facts, and reassure the customer that you understand his problem – it will get him "nodding" with you for the first time.

   If at this point you have to check or investigate, it may be necessary to call back; certainly you should avoid keeping him holding on for long. You need to explain exactly what will now happen and how long it will take (a promise you must then keep – "I will be back to you within an hour"). It will help the situation if you use your name and if possible assure him you will call him back personally. Anything less may sound evasive.

5. *Answering a justified complaint.* If possible, accept the blame and apologise unreservedly. Remember that the customer sees you in sales as sales person, production manager and invoice clerk; you personify for that moment the company. State what action you will take to put things right, even if your own action is merely to pass the complaint on (never downwards, however).

   It is useful to give some perceived concession if possible, but not too much. You should try to do more than the minimum needed to put things right. Thank the customer ("for bringing this to our attention") and follow it up.

6. *Answering an unjustified complaint.* If the customer is mistaken or has got the wrong end of the stick, be diplomatic. If it is a misunderstanding, you can blame yourself for not being clearer, and the instruction book, a letter, the invoice, etc. for being confusing. Try to allow him to correct himself and "save face", e.g. "Do you have the delivery note in front of you?" He may see his error before you have to point it out.

7. *Complaint follow-up.* You must always do whatever you promised to do for the customer and must advise whoever else needs to know about the complaint (via the complaint form). But there is something else to remember.

A complaint is a contact with a customer, often a very close one, and one initiated by the customer. It can often be developed from a complaining call to a contented, ordering call – if not immediately, then soon. The easiest way to achieve this is to follow the technique above, and then do something extra.

Make a follow-up note in the diary or record card to ensure that you (personally):

(a) follow up to see if his complaint has been dealt with, if it concerned another division;
(b) contact the customer to enquire if he feels the complaint was brought to satisfaction;
(c) refer to the (satisfactory) outcome at the next contact;
(d) verify his next order by writing a letter and making him feel that you have taken notice of him, that you really do regret customers having to complain.

91. Be appreciative

While you should never expect a customer's support you should show appreciation of business received. Customers do not, in any case, "support" you, they do business with you only because your product or service meets a need and does so in a way that offers better value for money than any competitor. Your professionalism, good service and expertise may, of course, be a part of the basis on which they make their decision. So too may their respect or liking for you, but to talk of support is the wrong way of putting it; certainly you should not say to a customer "Thank you for your support". (They may complete in their mind the corny old quip – "thank you for your support, I shall always wear it!").

Nor should you state thanks in a way that appears to grovel. Too much gushing thanks can be read as desperation for business and you do not want customers to see you in that light. Thanks must be clear, sincere and business-like. Thanks can be said, but may mean more if it is put in writing. It is pleasant to receive a letter that has been written for no other reason than to express thanks; apart from the fact of the thanks it shows respect for the customers and that you feel the business relationship is worth some trouble to maintain. And sometimes it needs to be more tangible – a drink or a meal may be appropriate. This can be positioned as a chance to relax together after the work and the decision that has been gone through, and is often better done in a way that rewards past customer loyalty and is not in danger of being seen as a bribe given with the hope of winning future orders.

Developing Repeat Business

A continuing relationship promotes a continuing flow of orders. But more of the same may not be achieving everything you can in terms of either revenue or profitability; increasing the levels of repeat business necessitates other approaches, for instance to sell the product or service range. Such are the topic of the next set of headings.

92. Achieving customer profitability

The concept of sales productivity has already been mentioned, the more you achieve in terms of sales from customers the more productive you will be; it is always easier and may be less time consuming to sell more to people you already know than to find still more prospects. More sales, and particularly more sales across the range of products or services you sell will also increase profitability, though discounts sometimes given to larger or regular customers may reduce margins somewhat. Some analysis of customers, certainly of the larger or those who are potentially larger, is useful to see whether there are further possibilities to sell more over and above simply keeping in touch and maintaining contact.

There are two key factors to consider in such an analysis, which can be simply done; they are the product range and the different buying points in a particular customer. You will be familiar with the first, your product range may be simple – products A, B and C – or there may be greater complexity and you may do better to consider groups of products (in the way a publisher might divide their list of books into groups such as fiction and non-fiction, or into more detailed categories such as business books within non-fiction).

By different buying points I mean people – buyers – and also places: a customer may be organised in two divisions, both with a buyer for your products, or have offices in– several locations, or you may have opportunities to do business separately with two or more departments – marketing, personnel and administration perhaps.

It is comparatively simple to plot these two factors together on a matrix chart (see figure 5) which allows you to fill in either levels of business you are already doing, would like to do (potential) or look at their total sourcing for some product line. Such an analysis quickly shows where there are any gaps in your coverage, helping review whether you are seeing all the right people, and looking at what you are achieving with each.

		BUYING POINT A	BUYING POINT B	BUYING POINT C	TOTAL
P R O D U C T S	1				
	2				
	3				
	4				
TOTAL					

Figure 5: Matrix chart

This is specially helpful with large customers. A healthy level of business can disguise opportunities, you may look at the overall, large, revenue figure and simply say "good" – missing the fact that there are additional possibilities. Where the customer knows you, likes the product and contact is in any case continuing, this technique can be very helpful in focussing future time and effort with the customer and result in action plans that increase sales results.

The next several headings also investigate the idea of selling more to those you already know.

93. The "gin and tonic" technique

This description refers to the linking of one purchase with another and represents a simple and effective way of increasing sales. The name comes from the sale of drinks. Someone walks into a shop and asks for a bottle of gin, or whisky, vodka or whatever. The sales-orientated assistant should automatically ask: "How many mixers would you like?" and will very often sell a dozen bottles of tonic water in addition to the original item requested if they do so.

This idea has wide application. You have to work it out and experiment with the links that can be used in this way around your product range. The following examples will help you appreciate the point:

- razor blades and shaving soap
- pen and paper
- shoes and shoe polish
- strawberries and cream
- petrol and oil, for the car.

All these are retail purchases we might all be asked about as we shop. But there are other, more elaborate links of the same sort:

- opening a new bank account might be accompanied by questions about savings schemes or pensions
- machinery linked with spare parts and a service contract
- a car with insurance
- a computer system with software, or vice versa – and computer stationery
- a laser printer with a heavy duty unit for it to stand on
- an airline ticket with hotel accommodation or car hire.

Such a list can doubtless be considerably expanded. The additional purchase may be immediate, two items being bought together, or a second purchase may follow later. However it can be made to occur, it can be made to produce extra sales. All it often takes is a simple question. So watch out for all the possible links and use them. Make it a reflex and increase sales and do so with comparative ease.

94. Build on success

Most of your customers will be happy with you most of the time and, although a few may have the occasional complaint, let us assume this is the case. There will still be some moments when customer relationships are at an extra high point. Something has happened to make the customer think particularly well of you, your company or your product. This may include such things as:

- exceptional service (by you), including the efficient righting of an error
- particular satisfaction, for example your advice, product or service has solved or helped solve some problems, or let them take advantage of a timely opportunity
- experience of back-up service, something resulting in a saving of time or money perhaps
- something unexpected, a query they assumed would be troublesome, dealt with painlessly or a technical possibility they had not realised was available.

Many things may occur with customers you deal with regularly, and it is always worth your advancing follow up action or moving on to develop new initiatives at such a moment.

For example, a test of some equipment is arranged and, the satisfied customer places an order – that may be the moment to move on to selling more of the range. Customers are more likely to commit when they are pleased not just with you, but with themselves. At a time when business is good, your contact at an account has just been promoted or some initiative they have taken has worked out well, they could be a little more receptive to what you have been trying, perhaps with limited previous success, to interest them in.

95. Be a source of ideas

It is often not sufficient to be a professional, efficient representative. Customers expect more – certainly they like to find they get more. Positioning yourself as an advisor has already been mentioned, for some customers the way to really win their loyalty is to be seen as a source of ideas. It has been said of management that they are not paid to have all the good ideas necessary to run their part of the business well, but they are surely paid to make sure there are sufficient new ideas to keep up or keep ahead. Similarly with sales people and customers, you do need to be on the look out for any ideas that might help your customer's business – especially, of course, those that link to your product or its use.

For example, one salesman selling carpeting to refurbish an office area, extended the order by persuading the customer that the opportunity should not be missed to improve the look of the nearby reception and showroom area. The idea of how much more impressed their own customers would be when they visited them was seen as important, more important than the additional cost (and there were some savings that could be worked out by using the same carpet, rather than undertaking a separate job some time later).

Such things need an active, creative approach often necessitating being a little more involved in the customer's business. Some salesmen are very successful at this and get themselves into a position where customers telephone them – "What do you think about so and so" – consulting them at an early stage on areas of mutual interest. Such an approach thus has two benefits to the sales person, first, directly introducing new sales opportunities. And secondly, creating an atmosphere in which customers are more likely to come to you, to ask to involve you at an early stage, all of which may extend sales possibilities beyond the basic requirement.

Helpful Attitudes

We now move towards the end of this review with the topic with which we began, that of attitudes. Earlier we looked at the right attitudes to the sales process, now we look at the attitudes you bring to bear closer in, in terms of your deployment of the many methods and techniques involved. Look at it all in the way most likely to get you operating in the best possible way and make customer feel you are a professional person to do business with, and your sales may well increase.

96. Adopt a positive approach

Probably one of the oldest stories about a positive approach to selling is that which contrasts two salesmen's differing attitude to a glass partially filled with water. Asked to describe it, one did so by saying that it was half empty, but the other described it as half full. It is easy to say "be positive", more difficult to suggest to a pessimist how to take such a view. A pessimist has been described as someone who thinks things are going to get a lot worse before they get worse. If you really think like that perhaps you should not be in selling. Most sales people are optimistic by nature. So much so that it can be one of the reasons why certain elements of the sales job are neglected — planning and preparation being put optimistically on one side with the thought that somehow it will all be alright on the day.

Success does, to some extent, depend on attitudes and attitudes alone. The successful salesman does not entertain the thought of failure, but goes into every meeting convinced he can achieve the objectives. It is a question of belief. But let us consider two very practical points. Firstly, whatever techniques of personal hype you may go in for, there are a number of tangible factors from which this kind of positive attitude flows and many of them are topics of their own within this book.

For example, you will be more confident of success if you:

- know your customers and your product
- prepare
- anticipate customer's reactions

So think about what does help you in your kind of selling and make a mental note to utilise it in how you approach the sales task.

Secondly, you must *sound* positive. Customers notice anything less and will read it as a lack of certainty about the claims you make for your product. You should be saying:

- this *will* be the case . . .
- these *are* the reasons . . .
- it *is* a . . .

and not including in your conversation such phrases as;

- I think . . .
- and perhaps . . .
- it is possibly . . .
- maybe we could . . .

Small points perhaps, but if this line is pursued consistently throughout your conversation then the customer is going to see you as authoritative, having the courage of your convictions and believe you are setting out for them what you clearly believe and are prepared to demonstrate in the case.

Selling demands a positive approach, you operate better if you are thinking positively and you will come over in a better light to those with whom you deal. It is true; positively so.

97. Be distinctive

Before people will buy from you, certainly on any sort of regular basis, they have to *remember* you. And often sales people are all similar and frankly rather difficult to differentiate in either appearance or manner. There is, as a result, advantage in standing out, though you do have to be careful about doing so with gimmicks. There are sales people who appear to get away with outrageous gimmicks, but they have to be good to do so.

But some seem to make it work. I have met sales people who

always wore a bright bow tie, had oversize pink spectacle frames, wore a distinctive hat, drove an antique convertible Bently or always wrote everything in a fountain pen filled with green ink. I would not recommend unthinking copying in this sort of area. What works for someone else may be disaster for you, though if you have your own version of this and it works, do not let this put you off.

There is another approach to creating this necessary memorability, however, which bases a point of distinction on something more practical. For example, one of the jobs done by representatives in the airline industry, is that they must call on retail Travel Agents. They do so not only to see the manager, but must brief literally all the staff who have contact with customers. This is not an easy task in a busy office where telephones are constantly ringing and not everyone can pause in their work at one time. So, what one such representative did was to arrive mid-morning with a tray of drinks, tea and coffee, and a bag of donuts. By mid-morning people were ready for a break, they welcomed the interruption and he encouraged them to pause for a chat in two groups to ensure the office continued to function. He got the time he needed with everyone, the manager approved it as a way of keeping his staff up-to-date without much interruption, and a considerable impact was made. So much so that the trade all knew and spoke highly of what they called "the donut man".

Now that is creative thinking. It creates distinction, yet does so in context of the objectives, the way the business works and, not least, in a manner the customer approves. If you can think of ways that meet these criteria and that help you stand out then you may well become better remembered and be so for what are considered very much the right reasons. It does pay to stand out.

98. Ride out failure

The English actor and playwright Noel Coward once said (of a fellow writer): "That poor man. He's completely unspoiled by failure." As he said it he doubtless intended it as an insult, but there is the germ of a very good motto there for most of us in selling. Failure — a customer who says a firm "No" — is likely to be something that occurs regularly. In some kinds of selling the anticipated and actual failure rate is high; the highest I have come across was 99%, and in the company concerned that constituted hitting target and if everyone did so they all made a good living. Whatever you sell there will be a prevailing strike rate.

The first thing to be clear about is simply that it happens. You are not going to sell to everyone you ever meet and there is no merit in expecting otherwise. This does not mean, of course, that you do not set out with the intention of selling to everyone. No one likes getting the negative responses. Every single one hurts, and always will; indeed it always should. But that should not mean that you go into a fit of depression after receiving a "No", and it most certainly does not mean that you allow your next meeting to be reduced in effectiveness because you are extra worried about it.

You need to come to terms with the ratios. Every call has a chance of success. The job is to work in such a way that those chances are increased. On the other hand some, inevitably, will not result in an order and a few will result in an ego bruising brush off, and occasionally real rudeness. Never mind. If you work in sales then this "goes with the territory" as they say. A run of negative results is difficult to take, but an emotional response only makes the next sale more difficult. Analyse what went wrong by all means, think about it constructively, and make a point of learning from any identifiable mistakes. Remember too, there will not always be a mistake, some buyers are never going to buy your product no matter what you do. But do not just dwell on any failure and allow yourself to become demotivated by it; confidence in what you do is important and you must not let this valuable commodity evaporate in a fit of anger or regret at one meeting that does not pan out the way you want.

Learn to bounce back from the misses and you will keep the strike rate up; and reduce the stress levels as well.

99. Be confident

It is easy to say "be confident", harder sometimes to comply. In part confidence is pure belief in yourself, and, as such, you are the only person who can cultivate it. If you totally lack confidence perhaps you should not be in selling. But confidence is also a matter of preparation (which has been mentioned) and experience.

Consider preparation first. There are many aspects of this that should raise your confidence, for instance if you:

- know your product
- know the customer and have done some research
- have clear objectives
- have thought through the kind of meeting you want to run
- have anticipated objections that may be raised
- prepare the aids for the meeting.

Prepare these factors and more, and the certainty that follows that some of the variables involved are no longer quite so unpredictable will bolster your confidence.

Not everything, and sometimes not very much, is predictable. Here experience comes in, you know you have a capacity to deal with most of the kinds of things that may occur. If you have been in selling for a while there is not so much that occurs that is totally new. Everything comes in unique form from the individuals who are your contacts and customers, but you know you have a facility for dealing with the various permutations. And you know (I hope) that you learn from experience, every call you make, every customer you talk to, should make you just a little more able to cope with the next and the next. Again all this is a source of confidence. Look for and use the things that are around which can increase your confidence and, whilst avoiding bravado which can stifle thought and consideration, approach every situation with the fullest confidence you can muster. Being confident is a habit. It can give you the edge on any competitor who, while perhaps as well qualified, is more hesitant about their ability to do what is necessary to succeed.

100. Learn from experience

An attitude that prompts you to learn from experience is valuable in any activity where you strive for excellence. In selling it is a very real asset. Selling, as has been referred to previously, is a dynamic activity, yet it can be repetitive. It is very easy to get into a rut and find you are repeating all the ways you have developed regardless of whether they remain valid or not. This is made more likely by customers. It is said that selling gets worse with practice. As customers respond, any negative tone to their response tends to lead to a dilution of sales effort as people tend to play it safe, going for what is least likely to upset customers rather than for what will be most likely to convince them.

On the other hand the sales job inherently has the ability to build up experience in a marked way. Many sales jobs involve 1000 or more customer meetings every year. Every one potentially holds surprises, opportunities to experiment and learn from the way things go. This means watching for things that are not quite as you would wish, and also noting those things that go well so that they can be repeated and developed further.

This approach must be maintained. You must never be complacent and believe that you know all about selling and do not have to worry about it any more. Everyone in selling spends a lifetime learning about it, refining it and adapting what they do to present and future conditions. The right attitude to this makes possible the fine tuning advocated in point 3, it also makes the sales job more rewarding, more likely to produce the results you want — and more fun.

101. Plan ahead

What of the future? Selling is likely to become increasingly complex as the market and individual customer attitudes change. You will have a fair idea of what makes for success in your sort of selling at present, and of what causes the difficulties. Let us review the key elements.

Selling is a form of communication, albeit persuasive communication. Good salesmen are good communicators and those skill need to be kept in good order. But research and preparation are important too. "Doing your homework" can be a differentiating factor and time must always be built in for. Selling is based on customer needs so you need to be able to find out successfully what your customers want and why, then you can match needs with benefits and sell on that basis, providing proof and evidence as necessary along the way. You must be able to handle objections, rebalancing the argument as you go along, and you must close — aim every time for a commitment from the customer that either secures the business or moves matters constructively forward.

You may also need less fundamental skills, account analysis and planning may be vital in your business, or major accounts or large individual orders may necessitate more sophisticated account handling and development skills. Other skills may be needed:

- to be equally persuasive in writing, with proposals or quotations;
- high level financial competence or negotiating skills; to be as effective in selling when on your feet in front of a group as you are one to one across a desk;
- to be expert at recognising real potential in prospects or excellent at selling a range of products,
- to be able to work productively and effectively.

There are no "magic formulae". But of two things you can be sure; first, the mix of skills that are necessary to success will change and, secondly, those who recognise the changing demands on them first will steal a march on their less predictive competitors. Whatever way your business is going it pays to be looking and planning ahead, watching for changes should ensure you see them coming, expecting to change will make it easier to do so.

102. Expect the unexpected

No, you are not mistaken, the title of this book does say "101 ways . . . "; but this extra one makes a useful final point. Selling needs – demands – a flexible approach, you never know what you are going to be faced with when talking to any individual customer. Some will be suprisingly difficult, or difficult in ways you did not expect, others will buy almost unprompted. The best sales people take everything that is offered to them and work to turn it to their advantage. If you assume the unexpected may well occur you will cope with it better. I wish you well with it all.

Afterword

Finally, to remind you that there really is a need to keep thinking continuously about ways to increase sales, let me quote a story reproduced from my book *Everything You Need to Know About Marketing* (Kogan Page) — a humorous look at marketing which sets out to demystify it for the layman. This story has been doing the rounds for more than twenty years, and I was told a version of it by my first sales manager; it makes a point and it goes as follows:

"Buyers are a tough lot.

It is any buyer's job to get the best possible deal for his company. That is what they are paid for, they are not actually on the salesmen's side, and will attempt to get the better of them in every way, especially on discounts.

This is well illustrated by the apocryphal story of the fairground strongman. During his act he took an orange, put it in the crook of his arm and bending his arm squeezed the juice out. He then challenged the audience offering £10 to anyone able to squeeze out another drop.

After many had tried unsuccessfully, one apparently unlikely candidate came forward, he squeezed and squeezed and finally out came a couple more drops. The strongman was amazed, and, seeking to explain how this was possible, asked as he paid out the £10 what the man did for a living. 'I am a buyer with Ford Motor Company,' he replied."

My sales manager finished it by saying: "Don't worry, buyers are not all really like that; most are worse!" Whatever you think of the people to whom you sell, they have a job to do, they want the right deal, they want value for money. Selling is helping them to buy. You must respect their view, and you must recognise that they are a "tough lot" — you need every technique you can find that will help you interest them, prompt them to buy and go on doing business with you in future. And they are ever changing, tomorrow their view and their demands will be different from today, you will need revised techniques to keep ahead of your competitors. As has been said a number of times through this text, recognising that is the first step to achieving it.